Learning about Biographies

Learning about Biographies

A Reading-and-Writing Approach
for Children

Myra Zarnowski
Queens College of the City University of New York

National Council of Teachers of English
1111 Kenyon Road, Urbana, Illinois 61801

National Council for the Social Studies
3501 Newark Street, N.W., Washington, D.C. 20016

For Eddie

NCTE Editorial Board: Richard Abrahamson, Celia Genishi, Richard Lloyd-Jones, Raymond Rodrigues, Brooke Workman; Charles Suhor, ex officio; Michael Spooner, ex officio

Staff Editor: Rona S. Smith

Book Design: Tom Kovacs for TGK Design

Cover Photographs: Gene Luttenberg, Accent Photographics

NCTE Stock Number 27789-3020

Library of Congress Cataloging-in-Publication Data

Zarnowski, Myra, 1945–
    Learning about biographies: a reading-and-writing approach for children/Myra Zarnowski.
       p.   cm.
    Includes bibliographical references.
    ISBN 0-8141-2778-9
    1. Biography (as a literary form)—Study and teaching (Elementary) 2. Heroes—Biography—Methodology. I. National Council of Teachers of English. II. Title.
CT22.Z37 1990
808'.06692—dc20
                                      89-48468
                                        CIP

Contents

Acknowledgments

Writing a book, as one fourth grader aptly put it, "is no piece of cake," but it does become manageable with the support of close friends and colleagues. I would like to thank a few of the many people at Queens College who have supported my efforts. Susanna Pflaum, dean of the School of Education, and Elaine Chapline, chair of the Department of Elementary and Early Childhood Education, encouraged me from the very beginning to pursue my interest in biography. I am especially grateful to Sydney Schwartz, professor of early childhood education, who generously took the time to read and respond to early drafts and later rewrites.

Without students, ideas about teaching and learning are just unrealized possibilities. My friends and colleagues at P.S. 201 in Flushing, Queens, enabled me to try out each of the strategies discussed in this book. I would like to thank Norm Sherman, principal of P.S. 201, whose first response to my idea for a biography project was, "Anything is possible." I would also like to thank Lila Alexander and Milly Sturman, two teachers who generously welcomed me into their classrooms, not for just a few days or a few weeks, but for an enduring collaboration that is now entering its fourth year.

Foreword

As an author of many biographies for children and adults, I think I have learned something about the craft of trying to re-create a human life on paper. Some of my knowledge comes from the long struggle to gather the facts and organize them into a narrative that penetrates the reality of the subject's life and opens the reader to a deeper understanding of experience. Some comes from close study of the long shelf of books about the art of biography, written by the practitioners themselves or by scholars in the field.

What is new about Myra Zarnowski's book is that it shows teachers in the elementary and middle schools how to use biography as a vehicle for developing children's natural curiosity about people and the world around them to the point where they themselves investigate a particular life and, through the artful use of language, tell that human story to others.

I have read Professor Zarnowski's book, of course, but before that, I had the good fortune to observe how she put its principles and methods to work in a classroom of some twenty-five students. Not a special class, not an elite group, but the typical mixed group to be found in a big-city public school. I saw her doing with wit, humor, and grace what she writes about so effectively. The students' zest for learning was manifest throughout the period.

The class was completing a three-month project built upon the life of Benjamin Franklin. Earlier they had listened to their teacher read aloud from several simple biographies of Franklin and had noticed on their own how different were the treatments of that story—from the facts selected by the biographers to the interpretation given those facts. The more they read, the more interested they became. From here—in stages that the book describes in detail—the children went on to do their own research on Franklin and his times and then to devise their own versions of a great American's complex life.

It seems plain that such creative work in the classroom can help children to understand how a biographer uses the freedom to select, to arrange, to depict a life from the mass of facts collected. And to understand at the same time what it takes to capture character in action, personality in performance. All this while acquiring basic skills in reading, research, and writing.

Few children will become professional biographers or historians. But through Myra Zarnowski's exercises they will come to realize how inseparable is the life from the times it is lived through. They will see more clearly how their world of today was shaped by the past and how human character develops under pressure. Perhaps they will understand too how writing biography, like writing history, is the creation of the collective memory.

—Milton Meltzer

Introduction

The immediate focus of this book is biography, a fascinating and often controversial subject. But the approach described here rests on broader, more far-reaching beliefs about the nature of teaching and learning. These beliefs stem from twenty years of classroom teaching, reading, and reflecting.

Chief among these beliefs is the importance of in-depth learning. This is learning about one topic for a considerable period of time. It is learning pursued with the zeal of a hobbyist or enthusiast for a chosen subject. An ardent baseball fan, a movie buff, an antique collector, or a model builder—these people maintain an intense interest in a subject for a period of years or even a lifetime. They are proud of their special knowledge and consider the effort involved in developing their expertise to be well worth it.

In a similar way, children can become keenly interested in their classroom learning if, like hobbyists or enthusiasts, they are allowed to spend large chunks of time learning enough about a subject to consider themselves experts. In the classroom this means abandoning a curriculum that hops around from topic to topic in favor of one that delves deeply into a few selected topics.

A second belief is in the value of manipulating the material that is to be learned. For years math educators have emphasized the importance of manipulatives for learning concepts. These can be rods, blocks, boards, or slices of cardboard pies. Science educators, too, have emphasized hands-on experimentation and observation. This is a productive path for history teachers, as well. But in the case of learning history, the manipulation that occurs is largely through language. That is, once historical evidence has been collected (e.g., documents, artifacts, reports, statistics, interviews), it is up to the student of history to organize it so that it makes sense. Through the process of selecting and grouping evidence, discussing it, and writing about it, children learn history and language skills at the same time.

And this leads logically to acknowledging the importance of listening carefully to what children have to say. If we ask children to make sense out of evidence, then we can learn a great deal about the way they think simply by listening to them. We can then try to fill in gaps in their understanding. At the same time we can offer them the opportunity for genuine conversation. We can ask genuine questions: How would you describe the subject you are studying? What makes you think that way? What is your strongest argument? Is there any contradictory evidence? What is the most surprising information you have found? Unlike contrived conversations that consist of questions asked to test students' knowledge, genuine conversations stem from a desire to know and a desire to share. When conversational partners listen and respond to each other's ideas, they are engaging in dialogue that promotes learning.

However, it is hard to reverse the seemingly logical practice of telling things to children all the time. After all, we have experienced more and read more. We have many things to tell. And while some amount of telling is quite informative and beneficial for children, uninterrupted telling is not. Uninterrupted telling is a one-way street, and the not-so-hidden message is that whatever children have to say is not worth listening to. So just as I learned, quite literally, to sit on my hands during writing conferences instead of grabbing my students' papers from them and "fixing" them up, so too have I learned to speak less and listen more. I have learned to value genuine dialogue.

Why, then, does this book focus on biography? The simplest reason is that using biography works. It gives children the opportunity to experience in-depth learning, manipulation of material, and genuine conversation.

I have seen this for myself. Several years ago I ran two classes in biography at the Queens College School for Children. Week after week, I saw that children between the ages of six and eight were interested in looking at picture book biographies and then discussing, drawing, and writing about the people described in these books. Even as they left class, I could hear them talking animatedly to their parents about Leonardo da Vinci, Mozart, or Peter the Great. Older children, aged nine to thirteen, enjoyed reading biographies independently, discussing them in small groups, and then drawing and writing about them.

This first positive experience encouraged me to move my efforts into an elementary school. I was fortunate in that two experienced teachers at P.S. 201 in Flushing, Queens, Milly Sturman and Lila Alexander, were willing to work with me in order to try out various approaches to reading and writing biography. Together we experimented with ways to help children assume the role of biographer with all of its joys and many of its frustrations.

We saw that children found this experience to be challenging and engaging. A majority of students reported that writing a biography was the longest project they had ever worked on. At the same time they described the experience as "very exciting," "fun," and "not boring." They had learned to do something they had never done before—something different, something special.

But there is an additional reason that this book focuses on biography. It is to help children learn about nonfiction literature. It is unfortunate but true that well-written biographies are resting all too peacefully on our library shelves. For without guidance, children rarely reach for these books, and when they do, they may not have sufficient background to understand them. The only solution to this problem is to actively teach children about biography.

This book, then, brings together my enthusiasm for biography and my belief in a particular type of classroom learning. The result is a reading-and-writing approach to biography.

I Understanding Biography

Part I provides background information for teachers who want to begin their own biography-centered programs. Chapter 1 examines the appeal, for both adults and children, of reading and writing biographies and discusses the value of biography in elementary and intermediate-grade classrooms. Chapter 2 looks at some practical and pedagogical considerations to keep in mind when choosing a subject for an in-depth biography project. Chapter 3 examines how children—and professional biographers—decide which information to include in a biography and considers how teachers can aid students in the critical evaluation of their materials.

1 The Appeal of Biography

When ten-year-old Flori finished writing a biography of Benjamin Franklin, she wrote this note on the last page:

About the Author

My name is Flori and if you are reading my book, note this. I wrote the book and illustrated the book myself. It was alot of hard work, but it was worth it. Please read, look at the pictures, and enjoy.

Flori was making several important points. The first point is that her book is original; while there are many books about Ben Franklin, none of them is exactly like hers. Second, writing the book was "hard work," requiring a great deal of reading, writing, discussing, thinking, and planning. There were also moments of uncertainty and frustration. Then, too, the work required large chunks of time—not days or weeks, but *months*. But because she now has something unique to share, she says it was "worth it."

One week after Flori completed her book, she told me she was interested in reading still more about Franklin. As she put it, "Each different book has its own way of explaining Ben Franklin's life." Flori has become an author and a critic of a specific type of literature—the biography.

Professional biographers describe their work with enthusiasm similar to Flori's. They refer to their activities as intellectually stimulating, often highly emotional, and frequently full of surprises. It is not, as some may think, a tedious pursuit among dusty documents in dimly lit corners of a library or an archive.

Biographers describe their research as intriguing, especially when they are pursuing a hunch or turning evidence this way and that in order to see it from a new angle. For example, Lyndall Gordon (1985), biographer of T. S. Eliot's early years, describes how exciting her research became as she began to find more and more evidence to support her "hunch":

These initial discoveries gave an irresistible momentum and direction to routine biographic research. I simply went ahead with a conviction that the truth would speak for itself. The excitement of detection drove me from one library to another, from Hamilton, Ontario to Charlottesville, Virginia. These journeys . . . were never tedious because this research had never been done so that there was always hope of a find. And, incredibly it seemed, at every library there *was* a find. (179)

Another reason for the biographer's enthusiasm is the special relationship that develops between writers and their subjects. This relationship, a friendship of sorts, becomes stronger and stronger over a period of time. After spending five years writing a biography of Dr. Martin Luther King, Jr., here is how Stephen Oates (1986) described his growing attachment to a man he never once had the opportunity to meet:

> I came to know King so intimately that I spoke to him in my dreams. I even fell into his speech rhythms when I talked about him in interviews and on the lecture circuit. Moreover, his teachings affected me personally. . . . In a strange and miraculous way, the very man I re-created became a warm, sympathetic friend. (137)

In a similar way, Flori recorded her growing attachment to her subject, Ben Franklin, in a journal she kept while she was gathering information. When she read about Franklin's stormy relationship with his brother and his desire to prove his superiority, she wrote, "He thought he was a better author than his brother [and] that was very funny because he is a mere boy. . . . I liked that part especially." When she read about Franklin's years with his wife, she wrote, "I like when they talk about opening a store, and they will give out pamphlets and other nice things." Much later, she added, "I feel sorry for Benjamin because in 1774 Deborah [his wife] died." Flori's comments, a mix of fact and feeling, show that she has become Ben Franklin's "sympathetic friend."

Biographers enjoy the intellectual challenge of their task. They are explorers trying to find new information and new explanations. When they begin, they never know what they will find or what they will think about their findings. David McCullough (1986) explains why biographers find these explorations so intriguing:

> I suppose it will take six years or more to write a book about Harry Truman. One subject. It isn't one subject. It's a thousand subjects. And the magic, the sense of adventure, comes from not knowing where you're headed or how you're going to wind up feeling, what you're going to decide. (47–48)

Flori shared these positive feelings about exploration. When I asked her why she read so many books about Ben Franklin, she replied, "I wanted to see how each one was told and make sure the facts I read in one book were correct." She was aware that she was reading not only facts but also someone's interpretation. Later, she commented that the reason that there were so many books about Franklin was that "many people might have thought differently about somebody's facts."

Not only do biographers spend years researching and writing, they also write passionately about the process of creating their works. Their descriptions of how they select their subjects, how they find their material, and how they present it make for fascinating reading. Even the titles of these process-centered books, titles such as *From Puzzles to Portraits* (Clifford 1970), *Biography as High Adventure* (Oates 1986), and *The Biographer's Gift* (Veninga 1983), suggest that biographers see themselves as problem-solvers, discoverers, and artists. They shape both their ideas and their language.

When children become biographers, they, too, experience intellectual excitement, surprise, and personal involvement in their reading and writing. Children who pursue a topic in depth do not lose interest. Easy-to-read books provide a framework of information that enables children to move on to more difficult materials. As they become more familiar with their subject, primary source materials (i.e., speeches, newspaper articles, and letters) become increasingly comprehensible and relevant.

For example, fifth graders who studied Eleanor Roosevelt found that letters addressed to her during the Great Depression showed how many Americans viewed her as a compassionate and accessible woman, someone they could appeal to for help. These letters only became significant and interesting once the children had a framework for interpreting them. This framework was their considerable knowledge of Eleanor Roosevelt's public career and their understanding of the Great Depression.

It is the powerful combination of *caring about* a subject and *knowing about* a subject that enables children to write biography with conviction and voice. As they read about a person, children not only learn information, they also develop feelings of sympathy and empathy, and sometimes anger and aversion. One fifth-grade student who studied about Eleanor Roosevelt wrote the following sympathetic response in her journal: "I felt so sorry for 'Little Nell' because she [was] punished all the time for stupid things." This sympathetic response is typical of the affective responses children make as they learn about the lives of historical figures. As they develop both emotional and intellectual understanding, children begin to strongly connect with figures from the past. Ultimately, these connections enable children to connect with the larger scope of history.

Since biography engages children and enables them to use language creatively, it is a particularly appropriate focus for elementary school language arts programs. This is because, as discussed next, the features of biography complement—or match—the needs and interests of elementary school children.

Biography and Elementary School Students: An Appropriate Match

Biography is appropriate material for children because it bridges what they already know and understand with what they need—and even *want*—to learn. This is so for several reasons. First, biography resembles other narratives children enjoy, making it an easy transition from fiction to history. Second, biography teaches children information about the world in an accessible, engaging way. Third, reading and writing biography teaches children about the role of interpretation in nonfiction writing. Children begin to realize that more than "facts" are involved.

Children Understand Narratives

Everybody likes a good story. Hearing the latest episode in a series of episodes provides entertainment while it feeds our curiosity. But for children, stories are more than just a form of entertainment. Stories provide the motivation to plunge ahead, to read and listen with purpose. Children want to know the answer to the ever-persistent questions: "What happened?" "And after that?" They want to know what the main character did from start to finish. "Then what?" The child's curiosity to find out how situations are resolved makes narrative the ideal type of material to engage children in literacy learning.

Biography is a unique type of narrative; it is the story of actual people and events rather than fictitious ones. Yet, in spite of all the "facts" found in biographies, biographers use many of the same techniques as fictional story writers. Biographers try to set their scenes descriptively, develop their characters completely, and give us the impression of life unfolding—all of this the way novelists and storytellers do. Because of these similarities between biographies and other types of stories children know and like, biography is a comfortable, somewhat familiar type of material for children.

In the following example, a child writing about biography makes use of what he already knows about narrative. Eight-year-old Jeffrey knows that in narratives something happens to someone. In his note to me about the picture book biography *Peter the Great* (Diane Stanley), he skillfully applies this knowledge (see Figure 1). Focusing his attention on the plot, Jeffrey writes mainly about Peter's dramatic actions. In fact, even though the setting plays an extremely important role in this story,

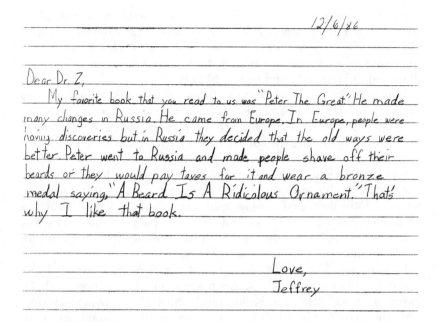

12/6/86

Dear Dr. Z,

My favorite book that you read to us was "Peter The Great." He made many changes in Russia. He came from Europe. In Europe, people were having discoveries but in Russia they decided that the old ways were better. Peter went to Russia and made people shave off their beards or they would pay taxes for it and wear a bronze medal saying, "A Beard Is A Ridiculous Ornament." That's why I like that book.

Love,
Jeffrey

Figure 1. Jeffrey, age 8, writes about biography.

Jeffrey only mentions it briefly. At the end of the note, Jeffrey includes a personal response to the book, explaining why it is one of his favorites. For Jeffrey, probing the plot is an easy starting point, an entryway into learning about biography and responding to it.

Life Histories Help Children Learn about the World

Biographies are written about people who have made an impact on society and who have overcome obstacles in order to do so. Most often—though not always—the impact is seen as a favorable one, one that benefited society. Consider, for example, the impact of the inventions devised by Benjamin Franklin, Thomas Edison, and Alexander Graham Bell. Educator and historian Diane Ravitch (1985, 79) suggests that when children read about such people, it puts " 'furniture' in their minds" enabling them to think critically and interpret other historical events. Without this "furniture," there is no plan for sorting any other related information a child may encounter. The learner simply doesn't know what to make of each new fact or what to connect it with.

Ravitch suggests that reading biographies not only builds historical understanding, but that children find this material fascinating. This claim is supported by the limited amount of available research dealing with children's responses to historical narratives (Levstik 1986a, 1986b). Children who are given the chance to select their own books do become increasingly interested and involved with the people and situations described in biography and historical fiction.

Why does this happen? Perhaps the best explanation is provided by Kieran Egan (1979, 1983a, 1983b, 1986a, 1986b). According to Egan, children during their elementary school years and even beyond are most interested in exploring the boundaries of achievement. The subjects of biographies, achievers of note, feed children's interest in understanding what is truly possible. In essence, as they read biography, children are learning about life by tapping the experiences of others. If it is possible for the people described in biographies to overcome obstacles such as ignorance, poverty, misery, fear, and hate, then it must also be possible for the rest of us. This is the very optimistic message that children find in biographies.

In addition, Egan (1986a) notes that the story form, which includes stories found in history, is a "sense-making tool" for children (250), "a haven of clarity" (248). The background information provided within a story shows readers how to interpret and feel about events that make up the plot. When a story ends and the conflicts are resolved, the reader knows who was good and who was evil. Similarly, after completing a birth-to-death biography, readers know if the subject was a hero (Martin Luther King) or a villain (Adolph Hitler). Readers feel enlightened, having learned meaningful information about life, and satisfied, knowing that the story has run its course.

In her journal, a fifth-grade girl highlighted the kinds of information found in a biography. She wrote with the insight of an experienced reader:

> Somebody who reads a biography feels that he has not just learned about the person but more of [the] country they lived in and the things [that] happened in their years.

Biography, as she points out, contains more than just the story of one individual. It contains the historical background necessary for understanding the person's life.

Writing Biography Invites Original Interpretation

Each year new children's biographies appear about such well-known figures as Christopher Columbus, George Washington, and Martin Luther King. In fact, just this week I read a new biography of Abraham Lincoln. While you might expect new biographies to cover the lives of contemporary people—Winnie Mandela, for example, is the subject of two recent biographies for children—what accounts for a new biography of Pocahontas or Alexander the Great? Why are these books being written? Why are they being read?

To answer this question is to probe the essence of biography as a genre. Writing biography requires not only research, but also insight and inspiration, for biography is not a collection of unorganized facts. If it were, the last bit of evidence a writer uncovered could be the last detail in his or her book; with enough information accumulated, a writer would simply stop working.

But that description fails to uncover what biographers actually do. While biographers *do* gather all the information they can, they also filter that information through their minds. Biographers are active decision makers, deciding what to include and what to omit, what to highlight and what to place in the background, and what to claim as truth and what to suggest as informed speculation. Biographers are interpreters of all the information they collect. This may account for the claim that, in effect, all biography is also autobiography. In the process of writing about someone else, biographers tell the reader about themselves and how they interpret the world (Westfall 1985).

To understand biography, a reader must understand the role of the biographer in selecting, shaping, and arranging the material. The writer's original design for a story has been described as "fact . . . rubbed up in the mind" (Kendall 1965, 17). The biographer is an artist who is able to bring together "a thousand thousand otherwise disparate facts and make them dance together" (Mariani 1983, 282). He or she does this by discovering a "theme which will bind all the important characteristics of the subject without omission or distortion" (Meltzer 1986, 174). Biographers agree that without this level of understanding it is not only impossible to make sense out of a collection of documents, tapes, note cards, and random intuitions, but it is impossible to make the subject come alive for others.

Intermediate-grade children can experience this process of interpreting and shaping historical material. When they do, they learn firsthand that biographers must create their own interpretations and make their own connections. One fourth-grade biographer explained the process she and her classmates used this way: "We used our imaginations with factual facts." In making this statement, she has acknowledged the creative aspect of biography.

Children who write biography also learn about reading. If biography is interpretation, then it is not as objective as it seems. It is easy, however, to mistake the unity of a work—the coherence or design created by the writer—with a false sense of objectivity (Nadel 1984). The work seems to unfold so logically, so inevitably. Yet for an experienced reader and writer of biography, this mistake should be less likely.

In fact, the wide range of possible interpretations of a life story is what accounts for the continuous stream of biographies about Columbus, Washington, and Lincoln. Each generation of readers and writers reinterprets history for itself. Nadel claims that "the need to rewrite a life when previous biographies exist is actually the recovery of one's freedom" (107). The new generation not only questions existing interpretations but also finds its own meanings.

When we encourage children to tell a life story in their own way, we are tapping both their language skills and their knowledge of story. We are showing them how to put language and story to work in order to make sense out of a collection of evidence left behind. We are inviting them to share in an intriguing process. When children accept the invitation, history becomes comprehensible, in-depth reading becomes engaging, and writing becomes an artistic endeavor. For these reasons, reading and writing biography are appropriate activities for elementary school students.

2 Choosing the Subject

Choosing a subject for a classroom biography project requires some thought. The "right" subject holds powerful appeal for children. Just how powerful was illustrated to me by an incident that happened in a fourth-grade classroom where students had been studying the life of Martin Luther King, Jr., for several months.

Without mentioning it to the children, the teacher switched their usual work time from 10 a.m. to later in the afternoon. At precisely 10 a.m., a hand shot up in the air and announced, "It's 10 o'clock. Isn't it time for Dr. King?" Several other children echoed the same question, also asking for their usual work time.

For this class, the time devoted to learning about Dr. King had become a predictable part of the day. They looked forward to it. But an even more important factor than predictability is that, even after months of study, these children continued to find their subject a fascinating one.

How can teachers choose subjects that children will continue to find fascinating? When making that decision, the writings of professional biographers provide us with considerable insight. Biographers tell us that the "right" subject is someone with whom the writer can form a special bond. According to author David McCullough (1986, 33–34), "a biographer must genuinely care about his subject, because as a biographer you're living with that person every single day." This sentiment is shared by Milton Meltzer (1986, 174), who states that a biographer "is thinking about the subject almost every minute of his waking hours, and frequently in his dreams." The subject becomes a constant companion.

When choosing their subjects, professional biographers also consider whether the subject's life was touched by major social issues. These issues might involve poverty or prosperity, opportunity or oppression, war or peace. If so, the life provides the author with a focus for examining these issues, "a means of illuminating the times and the great forces that shape the times" (Caro 1986, 226). In the process of showing how major issues affected the subject's life, the author enlarges and enriches the scope of the work, incorporating within it a slice of history.

Choosing a subject for in-depth class investigations like those described later in chapters 4 through 7 involves dealing with the same factors professional writers do. Any choice commits a class to examining one life and one set of issues instead of countless others. For the experience to be successful, there should be some reason to believe that the students will not only find the details of the subject's life fascinating, but that they will also be learning history.

For teachers, there are also practical issues to consider. Although there are many interesting subjects, not every subject is a good choice for classroom study. A good choice will meet curriculum needs by enriching existing programs or filling in gaps in what is taught and learned. The subject should also be one that children can research extensively, using a wide range of appropriate materials. Even the most interesting and relevant subject becomes an impossible choice when there aren't enough materials.

When considering a subject for a class biography project, it is helpful to try to build a strong case for your choice. Here are some questions that can guide your decision making:

1. Is the subject's life interesting enough to capture and hold children's attention?
2. Will a study of the subject's life bring children in contact with major issues and events in history?
3. Will children be learning about a historical figure who is unrepresented or inaccurately represented in textbooks and other curriculum materials?
4. Is there enough literature about this subject for children to read?

The next section illustrates how Flori's teacher, Mildred Sturman, and I used these questions to help us select Benjamin Franklin as the subject for a class biography project.

Selecting a Subject: Considering Ben Franklin

Is the life interesting enough to capture and hold children's attention?

A subject can capture children's attention if he or she accomplished something notable. Then one of the purposes that guides children's reading is discovering how the subject *did it*. This coincides with Egan's theory, mentioned in Chapter 1, that intermediate-grade children want to understand the "limits of what is possible" given the difficulties imposed by real-life situations (Egan 1986a, 251). Initially, the children want to know how the subject achieved success.

Ms. Sturman and I predicted that Franklin's life, with his many accomplishments, would easily capture children's attention. Although Franklin came from a rather ordinary family of modest means, during his life he managed to become quite famous for many extraordinary achievements. *How did he do it?*

We predicted that children would want to find out, that they would want to learn the stories behind his inventions. How did he invent the Franklin stove, the electric battery, and the lightning rod? We predicted that they would be curious about how he was able to initiate various civic improvements that changed the life of the citizens of Philadelphia. How did he organize the first lending library, the first volunteer fire department, and the first efficient postal system? And beyond these impressive achievements, we predicted that children would want to know how Franklin succeeded as a statesman and a diplomat. How did he influence the creation of the Declaration of Independence and the Constitution? How did he succeed as ambassador to France? How did he negotiate the final peace treaty with England?

How did he do it? We knew that children would find a number of explanations in their reading. First, Franklin was extremely hardworking. He perfected his reading and writing skills through intensive practice, using his own original methods. Second, Franklin had spunk. He was willing to take chances. When life as an apprentice became intolerable, he ran away to another state to start out on his own. When one opportunity fell through, he found another. In addition, he was intensely interested in things around him. He used this interest in science in order to better people's lives. Franklin was a man of both exceptional ability and persistence. One interpretation of his accomplishments is that they resulted from character traits he took great pains to develop. Of course, other explanations are possible.

Children's initial interest in biography is also captured by the conflicts that occurred during the subject's life. One powerful example is Franklin's stormy relationship with his brother James. During his youth, Franklin was apprenticed to James, a Boston printer. The two constantly fought, mainly because Ben wanted to contribute ideas and articles to the newspaper, while James wanted him to act more like a traditional, subservient apprentice. Ms. Sturman and I expected that children would be interested in learning the details of this conflict and finding out how it was resolved.

Initial interest develops into sustained interest only if the life story provides enough material to think about. As children read more, listen more, and discuss more about a subject, they become familiar with the basic life story. But, they want to hear it again and again—not the same books over and over, but different books about the same person. This is because they are becoming comfortable with a portion of history. In much the same way that preschoolers want to hear bedtime stories over and over again as they discover the world of literature, intermediate-grade students want to hear historical narratives again and again as they discover history. Once they have mastered the basic story, they are then able to reflect upon it. Their questions change from *What happened?* to the more imaginative *Why?* and *What if?* Their purposes for reading change, too. Instead of reading to find out what happened next, students read to find new "bits" of information and to confirm what they already know. Ultimately, they read critically to see how different authors tell the story.

Ms. Sturman and I realized that a study of Franklin's life would provide children with a great deal to think about. Because Franklin had been involved in science, government, writing, travel, and invention, children's research could branch off in a number of different directions. Since there were so many facets to Franklin's career, we predicted that children's initial interest in him would develop into sustained interest.

Will a study of this subject's life bring children
in contact with major issues and events in history?

A "good" subject leads children from the specific adventures of the person's day-to-day existence and into the larger context of history. As they read about a unique series of adventures, students are in a position to see the shaping influence of both time and place.

The story of *any* subject's life will show this influence of time and place. But a person who lived during a period of great social or political change (e.g., the Civil War or the Industrial Revolution), provides children with the opportunity to learn about major issues and events in history. The life story becomes a focus for this learning.

This idea has been clearly explained by historian and biographer Barbara Tuchman (1979), who refers to biography as "a prism of history" (134). Just as a prism takes in white light and breaks it into its component colors, so, too, a life "takes in" the effects of time and place and allows us to examine the resulting effects. Biography, according to Tuchman, becomes "a vehicle for exhibiting an age" (133).

Ms. Sturman and I felt that Ben Franklin could become such a vehicle for exhibiting his age. Through a study of his life, students would learn about the events that occurred during the onset of the American Revolution and the early years of the republic. As they followed Franklin's career as an agent of the colony of Pennsylvania sent to London, a member of the Continental Congress, an influential framer of the Declaration of Independence and the Constitution, and an ambassador to France and England, students would also be learning about significant events in American history.

Will children be learning about a historical figure who is unrepresented or inaccurately represented in textbooks and other curriculum materials?

As a means of teaching history to children, textbook material simply cannot "do it all." The notion that one book at a grade level can adequately cover vast stretches of time, vast geographic areas, and vast numbers of issues—all in a few hundred pages—is an unrealistic one.

In fact, the sorry state of textbooks used to teach elementary school social studies is hard to deny. In their review of primary-level textbooks, researchers A. Guy Larkins, Michael Hawkins, and Allison Gilmore (1987) describe the content of this material as "redundant, superfluous, vacuous, and needlessly superficial" (299). How can children learn important concepts from meaningless material? How can teachers derive challenging lessons from it? How can a passionate involvement with issues be kindled from sparse, uninspiring, and uninformative words?

And other researchers concur. Arthur Woodward, David Elliott, and Kathleen Nagel (1986), writing in *Social Education*, the primary publication of the National Council for the Social Studies, point out that the way elementary texts deal with important issues is "so scanty or disconnected that students find it difficult to understand the depth of passion these issues produced or their relevance to society today" (51).

In elementary school textbooks, the people who shaped history are treated superficially. That is, readers are told so little about them that they can hardly begin to feel sympathy or empathy—or form any other kind of bond with them. Larkins et al. (1987) point out that when two or three sentences in a textbook are devoted to Martin Luther King, Jr., for example, it hardly begins to explain the impact of his life on our society. That is why when a textbook is used, it needs to serve as a basis for further inquiry—inquiry that makes use of the growing body of high-quality nonfiction literature for children.

Children are interested in knowing more about the people who are mentioned in their textbooks. The problem is that their textbooks just aren't telling. Researchers Elliott, Nagel, and Woodward (1985) report that when they interviewed children about social studies textbooks, they heard comments such as, "Sometimes they just mention a person's name and then don't talk about them anymore in the whole book" (22). Children's textbooks race across history, often raising more questions than they answer. Children are understandably confused by this sketchy material.

Surprisingly enough, even the imposing figure of Benjamin Franklin has been given superficial treatment in textbooks. Larkins et al. (1987) report that in one textbook dealing with "the community," only Franklin's achievements at the local level are mentioned. The reader learns nothing about his career as a diplomat or statesman because it doesn't coincide with the narrow scope of the book. In addition, Franklin's entire career is dealt with in a mere 150 words.

For the students in Ms. Sturman's class, there was good reason to begin a study of Benjamin Franklin. A biography project would serve as a means of extending their ongoing study of American history. Nowhere in their textbook was Franklin presented as the extraordinary figure he truly was. It would only be through in-depth study that children would be in a position to develop a more balanced view of Franklin and a more complete understanding of the times in which he lived.

Is there enough literature about this subject for children to read?

For professional biographers, looking through literature and related documents is only a part of a larger set of research strategies. Biographers often travel extensively while completing their research. Some, like Samuel Eliot Morison, biographer of Christopher Columbus, retrace the paths of their subjects. Morison actually sailed the same routes Columbus did. Other biographers travel to their subject's birthplace, studying the setting firsthand and interviewing the subject's family, friends, and acquaintances. Robert Caro, biographer of Lyndon Johnson, actually moved to the Hill Country of Texas in order to better understand Johnson's background. On a more modest level, biographers frequently travel to special library collections, archives, and museums.

In contrast, elementary school students must rely heavily on literature as their major source of information. Since children cannot travel extensively, the books they use and the primary sources they examine must provide them with the information they need in order to understand the events in a life story. We must be careful to select books written in an interesting way, with a style that makes children want to keep reading. The books we provide should be examples of the best nonfiction writing currently available.

A class project requires that enough books be available for all students to read at the same time. This means having considerably more books than students. The teachers I have worked with and I have largely gathered this material from local libraries. In addition, a class project requires books at various levels of difficulty, ranging from picture books to sources that assume the reader already has a great deal of background information to draw on. Even very competent readers may want to begin their reading with short, "easy" books in order to get an overview of the subject's life. This overview can then be filled in by reading more detailed accounts. For less competent readers, picture book biographies provide an essential introduction to background information and vocabulary words. These books serve as stepping-stones to more challenging material. This is because once children master the basic life story, they find that the more difficult material does not contain a high percentage of "new" information. In fact, content becomes largely predictable and, therefore, manageable. It is fascinating to watch children work their way up to comfortably reading a book they once considered too difficult.

As we were in the process of gathering literature for Flori's class to read, Ms. Sturman and I were impressed by the number of books that described Ben Franklin's career. Using the public libraries in our area, we were able to locate biographies that were new and those that had been written more than forty years ago. Frequently, we were able to locate multiple copies. These books varied from the beautifully illustrated classic picture book *Benjamin Franklin* by Ingri and Edgar Parin d'Aulaire to Jean Fritz's humorous account of Franklin's inventions entitled *What's the Big Idea, Ben Franklin?* Besides the variety of picture book biographies and brief accounts, we were able to locate longer, more detailed works. To this we added some primary source material, material that had not been interpreted by any biographer or historian. Franklin was a prolific writer. Besides his famous *Autobiography*, he produced *Poor Richard's Almanac*, wrote ballads and even a skit, contributed to newspapers, prepared scientific reports, and wrote numerous letters. With all of this literature available to us, we were confident that we had enough material for all the students in the class.

A "Good" Subject

Our experience ultimately confirmed for us that Ben Franklin was a good subject for children to learn about. Almost from the start, Ms. Sturman's students connected with Franklin, becoming especially sympathetic to his problems with his older brother. They also remained interested in his career and his accomplishments during the three months we read and wrote about him.

The children's comments show us how they felt about becoming biographers of Ben Franklin. Here is what one fourth grader wrote at the end of his biography:

> I started writing this book in March and here I am in June still writing it. And believe me this is no piece of cake. I have to write it over and over until I get it right. It's taking me a long time, but it's worth it.

Another student wrote:

> I'd like to have been there when Ben Franklin was alive because his life sounds interesting. . . . I felt good writing this book because I got to know more about Ben Franklin.

A third commented:

> I enjoyed writing this book very much. I also found out things I didn't know.

What these children are saying in their comments is that the experience of becoming biographers was truly educational. Because writing a biography was not too easy ("no piece of cake"), it gave them a feeling of accomplishment ("it's worth it"; "I felt good writing this book"). In their reading, children found information that was new, not needlessly redundant ("I also found out things I didn't know"). A subject that promotes this type of learning is clearly a "good" one.

In addition to Ben Franklin, there are many, many other excellent subjects for classroom study. The questions offered in this chapter are designed to focus your attention on selecting a subject suited to your own unique goals, students, and resources.

Once you have selected a subject for a biography project, it is time to consider procedures for helping children gather information. The next chapter discusses how to help children select the material to include in their biographies.

3 The Material Included in a Biography

It is up to the biographer to decide what to include in a biography. Life writers have a great deal of freedom. But, at the same time, they are expected to tell *the truth*. The biographer's freedom is reined in by the responsibility to treat the subject fairly and honestly.

Children understand this to some extent. Intermediate-grade children do have criteria for selecting biographic material, and teachers who listen carefully to them can discover their assumptions.

This chapter examines children's descriptions of how they select material and then considers how teachers can support children's efforts to critically evaluate material.

Reading with a Critical Stance

Making Selections: Possibilities

When I asked fourth- and fifth-grade biographers how they selected their material, their responses were surprisingly similar. Over and over again, they talked about including just "the important information" and leaving out the rest, "something nobody thinks about." They stressed that there was a hierarchy of information and emphasized that they were the ones determining it ("I use my own judging"). Confidently, they discussed separating the important from the unimportant.

Nicole, a fourth grader, told me how she selected details, those nuggets of specific information she enjoys knowing*:

> *I pick out the important parts.* . . . I'm looking for mostly details that I can include in my book. Cause I like putting a lot of details into everything. . . . In the bus boycott [section] I put [in] a detail that said besides that Rosa Parks was arrested, she was also photographed, fingerprinted, and fined exactly $14. I like looking for those little details that not many people include in their books.

When I asked her how she decided which details to include, she answered me with a question:

---

*Here and throughout this chapter, italics have been added to student work.

> Is it really, really important enough to put in a biography? If it's
> not that important, then why should I put it in? It depends on the
> detail it is. *I use my own judging if it's an important detail or not.*

Paula, a fifth grader, agreed. In addition to explaining how she sorted
the information she encountered into two categories, important or
unimportant, she also talked about her desire to guide her readers'
understanding. She wanted to bring her readers into line, so that they
would see things the way she did. This is how Paula described the
procedure she used when writing about George Washington:

> What I do is, in my mind, I put in two sections. One section [is]
> hey, this is important, Paula, and one section [is] naaah, you don't
> have to keep that.
> When I was writing the first part of my biography, I remembered
> the terrible things that the soldiers went through during the war
> and I said, *"That's important, and that's what I want the readers to
> know—that's important."*

When children like Nicole and Paula read about the same subject—
George Washington, for example—their reactions will be alike in some
ways and different in others. This is because reading is an interpretive
event. To this interpretive event, or transaction, the reader brings his or
her background experiences, concerns, and ways of understanding the
world; the printed text supplies the symbols to be interpreted. The
resulting transaction between reader and text produces meaning and
response (Rosenblatt [1938] 1983, 1978, 1985).

Because readers do not all interpret a text the same way, some meaning is shared among readers and some is not. Purves (1985) refers to the
former as the "central tendencies" and calls the latter "dispersion." For
example, a fifth-grade class studying George Washington's career prior
to the American Revolution agreed that he was (1) well organized, (2)
used to directing a large number of people, (3) loyal, and (4) experienced
as a soldier. Some children saw these traits and experiences as important
factors that prepared Washington to become commander in chief of the
American army. Others thought that Washington was prepared to
become commander, but not because of these four reasons. Still others
thought that Washington was quite unprepared for the job. The "central tendencies" included the children's agreed-upon perceptions and
assessments of Washington's character and experiences. The "dispersion" involved the significance attached to these perceptions.

There are a number of reasons for encouraging children to give a wide
range of responses when they study people and events in history. First,
the writing that results, a combination of central tendencies and dispersion, is more interesting. Instead of a class set of nearly identical sum-

maries of other writers' ideas, each piece of writing will in some respects be unique. Second, it is more motivating—and more purposeful—for children to write about ideas that they hold with conviction. And finally, while all types of writing assignments support content learning, writing assignments that encourage students to make their own connections and to reason for themselves promote learning that is more thorough and longer lasting (Langer and Applebee 1987).

Making Selections: Problems

There are good reasons for encouraging young biographers to select their own material and respond to it, but there are also problems inherent in the approach. The most persistent problem is bias. What happens when a biographer discovers something unpleasant or shocking or something that simply doesn't seem quite right? Can it be left out?

Joseph Lash, the well-known biographer of Eleanor Roosevelt, faced this problem. One, while researching in the Franklin D. Roosevelt library at Hyde Park, he discovered some letters Mrs. Roosevelt had written that he considered to be unquestionably anti-Semitic. These letters did not fit in with his perception of Mrs. Roosevelt as an extraordinarily compassionate, loving person. Lash reports that since the library was about to close, he put the letters aside, "hoping somehow that overnight they might vanish" (1982, ix).

Similarly, historian and biographer Barbara Tuchman reported the shock she felt upon discovering that her subject, "Vinegar Joe" Stilwell had used language she considered extremely offensive. Stilwell, the American commander of the Allied forces in the Far East during World War II, had referred to FDR as "Rubberlegs." When Tuchman finally decided to include this term in her biography, "it felt like picking up a cockroach" (1979, 144).

Professional biographers like Lash and Tuchman ultimately make the decision to include disturbing material. Lash claims that such material strengthens a biography because it forces the biographer to embrace the ambiguities, irregularities, and inconsistencies in a person's life. Tuchman finds that, in the end, her responsibility as a historian outweighs her personal disgust.

But what about the biases children bring to the task of writing biography? Children are as prone as anyone else to leave out what they do not want to deal with. While they are less likely to come across shocking or revolting information, they are more likely to omit what they describe as "boring." That may mean emphasizing what interests them—usually issues related to childhood (school, parents, friends,

growing up)—while de-emphasizing more adult concerns (public service, career goals, diplomacy).

Biographies of Ben Franklin written by the fourth graders I worked
with clearly emphasized Franklin's childhood. The children's biographies sparkled with episodes about sibling rivalry and family devo-
tion, but were sparse when it came to discussing Franklin's diplomatic
career.

Similar omissions and even alterations occurred in fifth-grade biographies of Eleanor Roosevelt. One fifth grader went to great pains to
deny that Eleanor was a plain-looking girl, even though this detail was
mentioned many times in the books she read and she had seen a number
of photographs of Eleanor. This child sidestepped the problem when
she wrote, "I think Eleanor wasn't pretty and wasn't ugly. Eleanor was
not that ugly after all."

A few children were aware of the problem of telling a biased story and
talked about the dangers involved in omitting material. Referring to
why she included information about George Washington's marriage to
Martha Custis, one youngster said, "I had to put that down because it's
part of his life, and if you leave it out it messes up the whole story." This
youngster's concern for telling a well-formed story enabled her to
embrace the historian's concern for accuracy.

In addition to the problem of leaving out material, an equally distort-
ing influence on biography is the urge to create. The writer makes up
events or manufactures data where none exists. It is wishful thinking
gone out of control. Bernard Malamud (1987) describes this tendency
beautifully:

> In grammar school, where I lived in a state of self-enhancing
> discovery, I turned school assignments into stories. Once I married
> off Roger Williams of Rhode Island to an Indian maiden, mainly
> because I had worked up an early feeling for the romantic. (602)

One student writing about Eleanor Roosevelt also changed Mrs.
Roosevelt's life story to make it more to her liking. Angry at the way
Eleanor's mother ignored her, the youngster created this piece of wish-
ful thinking:

> Eleanor helped a lot of people, when her husband died. Since she
> was his wife, maybe what he was going to do, she did it for him.
> Even though she was a shy lady, she did it anyway. *I am very proud
> of her. If her mother were alive she would have been proud of her,
> too.*

In between the dual perils of self-imposed censorship and self-
commissioned fictionalizing lies the work of the biographer who tries to

interpret events fairly. Even young writers can be made aware of the dangers of biased reporting. As they try to avoid distortion in their own work, they can also look carefully and critically at the work of other writers.

Looking Critically at the Works of Others

Since elementary school biographers rely heavily on secondary source material, they need to be aware of the criteria for judging the biographies they read. Three features that are especially important when considering the authenticity of a work are (1) evidence of research, (2) evidence of a balanced portrait, and (3) evidence of real rather than fictionalized conversations. Children can learn to recognize these features and use them as a guide for selecting material to put in their biographies.

Finding Evidence of Research

The authors of carefully researched biographies for children leave tracks their readers can follow. These tracks show the path a writer took in order to write the book. Where did she go? Whom did she talk to? What did she see? In notes, postscripts, and appendixes, authors show their readers where their information came from. Some authors even remind their readers, as did Milton Meltzer in *Dorothea Lange: Life through the Camera*, that all biography is, in essence, "how one person sees and tries to understand another person's life and work" (58).

Teachers and children can examine several biographies together, looking for indications of the author's research efforts. In time, children will learn to look for these indications by themselves.

In *Lincoln: A Photobiography,* the 1988 Newbery award-winning book, author Russell Freedman lets the reader in on his research strategies. He acknowledges the people who helped him, lists the sources of the many quotations and photographs he used, recommends related books about Lincoln, and suggests places to visit in order to learn more. The reader gets the impression that Freedman has immersed himself in material about Lincoln, and the book jacket confirms that he has visited all the major Lincoln sites.

A number of biographers emphasize how their travels have helped them learn. Barbara Mitchell, author of *Raggin': A Story about Scott Joplin*, reports traveling to a ragtime festival to watch a raggers' competition and speak with the judges and organizers. R. R. Knudson, biographer of athlete Babe Didrikson, tells her readers of her trip to Beaumont, Texas, Babe's birthplace, in order to pound the pavements of

Babe's neighborhood and look at her trophies and memorabilia. Knudson even tried to match some of Didrikson's records for throwing a baseball, shooting free throws, and driving a golf ball. She lists these records and invites the reader to try to and match them, too.

Still other writers are fortunate enough to interview their subjects. Milton Meltzer reports that he knew Betty Friedan long before he wrote about her but had not seen her for years. However, before writing *Betty Friedan: A Voice for Women's Rights*, he not only spent time at Radcliffe College reading Friedan's papers, he also spent several hours interviewing her. Doris Faber, author of *Margaret Thatcher: Britain's "Iron Lady,"* tells her readers that she tried in vain to meet with Mrs. Thatcher and members of her family. Reluctantly, the author had to settle for traveling around London, watching Mrs. Thatcher on television, talking to reporters who dealt with her, and reading relevant newspaper accounts.

Biographers who tell their readers about their research make their writing more credible. We are more likely to believe a writer who has read, traveled, and interviewed as a means of learning than one who writes from unidentified sources.

Finding Evidence of a Balanced Portrait

A well-written biography provides an evenhanded treatment of the subject, telling about the subject's shortcomings as well as his or her achievements. Balanced portraits are becoming more and more common in children's biographies, and they can be pointed out to students. Once one or two of these accounts are brought to their attention, children will learn to question a biography that is only laudatory.

A balanced account like the one provided by Jean Fritz in *And Then What Happened, Paul Revere?* shows readers that Revere was inventive and talented, but also forgetful; on the night of his big ride, he forgot his spurs. R. R. Knudson tells us in *Babe Didrikson: Athlete of the Century* that Babe was an extraordinary athlete but overly competitive and self-centered. She annoyed her teammates by constantly bragging and playing her harmonica. In *Dorothea Lange: Life through the Camera*, Milton Meltzer explains that Lange's well-known photographs of migrant workers taken during the Great Depression showed her sensitivity to their suffering. At the same time, Lange was remarkably insensitive to her own children's needs. When authors write balanced accounts like these, they produce believable portraits. They show the complexity of human character and give texture to their work.

Balance does not imply debunking or going to great lengths to show negative qualities and false ambitions. It implies that the author tries to give a complete picture, one that makes the subject come alive. When reading, children can look for surprising details that cause them to pause and think. These are the details that make a writer's work distinctive, original, and memorable.

Finding Evidence That Conversations Are Real

Probably the biggest challenge to authentic information is the imaginary conversations found in children's biographies. These conversations may help the writer move the plot along or show the character in action, but they are all too frequently unbelievable and unproven.

For example, in Paul Walker's recent biography of Roberto Clemente (*Pride of Puerto Rico*), when Roberto tells his father that he lost a baseball game, his father replies,

> There are other boys and other teams, but there is only one life. I want you to be a good man. I want you to work hard. And I want you to be a serious person. (5)

Wouldn't a more believable response be, "Gee, that's too bad; better luck next time, son"? The writer never tells us where, if anywhere besides his imagination, such dialogue comes from. The author also sees into people's heads and reports the thoughts of both Roberto's high school teacher and a recruiter for a company softball team.

In contrast, *The Story of Pocahontas, Indian Princess* by Patricia Adams begins with a statement informing the reader that all the dialogue in the book has been researched and that nothing has been made up.

Fictionalized biographies can be interesting to read, but authors are responsible for informing their readers where fact ends and conjecture about *what might have happened* begins. This information prevents readers from finding fictionalized biographies a confusing mixture of fact and fiction. Informed readers can then discuss the effect of using fictionalized dialogue—whether it makes a biography more convincing or interferes with the development of the story.

As children learn to look critically at biographies, they will recognize which sources can be used with confidence and which with great hesitation. But more is involved in writing biography than pulling out facts. Biographers have a special way of looking at their material, a way that makes writing a biography an art.

The Biographer's Unique Stance

Biographers take a unique stance, or critical attitude, toward the material they discover while researching. This stance combines two strong concerns. The first is with the accuracy of the information they uncover: Why should a piece of evidence be believed? What is its source? The second concern is with pursuing an original interpretation of material: What is the significance of this evidence? What does it mean to me?

Children who learn to critically evaluate the biographies they read in terms of research, balance, and authentic conversation are taking a significant step towards adopting the biographer's first concern. And the biographer's second concern is already noticeable in the comments made by children who see themselves as judges and evaluators.

When biographers write, they combine their concern for accuracy with their concern for pursuing an original interpretation. When selecting material, a biographer will ask two questions: Is it true? Is it important to my understanding? The answers to these questions form the basis of all biography.

Gathering Information and Writing It Down

A great deal of writing occurs before the first draft of a biography is written. It occurs as professional biographers read, respond, and question the information they find. Biographers use a variety of formats depending largely on personal preference. Some writers fill hundreds of note cards that they later shuffle and sort; others file their data in manila envelopes; and still others write on large butcher paper that they eventually cut apart, sort, and tack to the wall (Lomask 1986).

Children also need formats for writing down information, responses, and questions that occur to them as they research their subject. Several procedures and written formats have been used successfully with young biographers who are in the process of gathering material. They include (1) writing group responses, (2) writing individual responses, (3) preparing group data charts, and (4) making trial runs. These strategies are infinitely reusable. They are used extensively in the long-term projects described later in chapters 4 through 7.

Writing Group Responses

During the early stages of a biography project, children gather material by listening to the teacher read aloud from a biography of the subject being studied. Since much of the material is likely to be new, there is usually a great deal that needs to be discussed and clarified.

After approximately twenty minutes of oral reading and discussion, the teacher and children create a written response together on large chart paper. First, the teacher asks the children to suggest information that they think is important enough or interesting enough to remember.

Martin Luther King, Jr.
by Doris and Harold Faber

Facts	Feelings
1. When he was little, things changed [for him] because of the color of his skin.	1. I thought it wasn't very nice. It was unfair.
2. He was learning about segregation.	2. I'd like him to feel like a normal kid.
3. M.L. remembered having to stand on a bus even though there were empty seats in the white section.	3. I think it was thoughtless. It wasn't nice. He was tired. M.L. said it was the angriest he ever felt.
4. He got shot. I thought it was on a train. I know it was a balcony now.	4. I don't know why he got shot when he was just fighting for freedom.

Figure 2. Responding as a group.

Then the children are asked to respond to this information, giving their thoughts and feelings. These items correspond to the biographer's two primary concerns—accuracy of information and original interpretation.

When a fourth-grade class began studying the life of Martin Luther King, Jr., their teacher took down the children's notes and comments. Figure 2 shows a portion of the chart they created together based on their reading of a book by Doris and Harold Faber. Even in this brief excerpt, it is evident that students were able to recall information, recast it in their own words, and respond to it. At least one student clarified a misconception.

Writing Individual Responses

The experience of responding as a member of a group eases children into the less-structured task of responding individually. Once students have listened to one or two books read aloud, they are given time each day to read independently and respond in a journal.

When given time and encouragement to write, children use their journals for a variety of purposes. Some remain true to a facts-and-feelings approach, as in the following example:

> While Martin was standing on the balcony outside his motel room,
> Dr. King was assassinated. People all over the world were shocked,
> angry and sad. I feel the same way because it was beginning to get
> peaceful and Martin made it happen. [corrected for spelling]

Some record anecdotes like this one:

> Once he and some friends walked into an elevator in a tall New
> York building. A woman got in the elevator, and mistaking King
> for an elevator operator said, "Six please" because M.L. wore a
> black tie and a black suit. It is funny because the woman probably
> did not look at his face. Or did not go in the Washington, D.C.
> march. [corrected for spelling]

Others critique the books they read:

> Well, the book just got to it. First, the author jumped to it. Then,
> catch, the first thing I read was when Washington was being elected
> for office.

A number of children squirrel away facts that might come in handy
later:

> Number 3 Cherry Street [was] the Manhattan house where Wash-
> ington was living during the first year of his presidency.

The journal is a place for storing facts, quotes, questions that arise,
feelings, and hunches—anything that might come in handy later.

Preparing Group Data Charts

Group data charts are introduced by the teacher in order to direct the
group's thinking and attention. The purpose of the chart is to help the
group collect the kind of information they will need when they begin
writing biographies. Data charts help make the task a manageable one.
The information in the chart is so important that collecting it becomes
a class effort done under the teacher's guidance.

One example will illustrate how group data charts support the efforts
of young biographers. A group of children who were studying the life of
George Washington were challenged by their teacher to decide if
Washington's earlier life prepared him to become commander in chief.
In order to decide, a chart was constructed to record information relevant to either position—"prepared to be commander in chief" or
"unprepared."

Each time the teacher read aloud to the students or the students read
independently, the teacher wrote down information the group felt was

George Washington as Commander in Chief

Prepared	Unprepared
1. At 21, he led a Virginia regiment against the French.	1. He never trained to be commander in chief.
2. He was big (over 6 feet tall) and very strong.	2. He had no formal education in England.
3. He always wanted to be a soldier like his brother.	3. He didn't like the woods.
4. As a surveyor, he camped out in the wilderness and learned how to survive there.	4. His real goal in life was to be at Mt. Vernon and run the farms.

Figure 3. Portion of a data chart.

relevant to either position. Figure 3 shows a small portion of what grew into a very large data chart.

The completed chart enabled the children to make an important interpretive decision and to support that position in writing. This is because the evidence to be evaluated—evidence that the group considered relevant—was in front of them while they were deciding and writing.

Making Trial Runs

Trial runs are writing experiences done with the support of the teacher. These experiences parallel the kind of writing the children will ultimately be doing by themselves. The experience focuses children's attention on the kinds of decisions they will be making.

One trial-run strategy that I have often used involves learning about the different ways to begin the biography. First, we examine published biographies and note and discuss the various ways to begin. Then children "try out" each type of beginning. Figure 4 shows some of the strategies that have been discovered and some examples of opening sentences written by fourth graders.

Other trial runs can be more elaborate, involving class collaboration in order to plan and write lengthier pieces. In every case, the purpose of a trial run is to walk children through a process they will later be using independently.

Ways to Begin a Biography

Strategy	Example
Direct Approach: Tell the reader what the section is about.	Fifty-nine years ago there were Jim Crow laws that separated blacks and whites.
	When Martin Luther King was little, there were Jim Crow laws.
Question: Ask a question and then answer it.	What were the Jim Crow laws?
	Why were there Jim Crow laws?
Description: Let the reader see what is happening.	Bathrooms for blacks were dirty and separate.
	Blacks had to sit in a separate section.
Startling Statement: Surprise the reader.	Martin Luther King's house was bombed. Why?
	Martin Luther King was shot.

Figure 4. Openings produced during a trial run.

The procedures for selecting and recording material described in this chapter are not ends in themselves. Instead, they come alive only when they are used to help children achieve real goals. Part II of this book concentrates on applying these procedures in order to achieve the very real goal of writing a biography.

II Biography in the Classroom: Approaches for Beginners

Part II describes four strategies for using biography in the classroom. Each strategy helps children confront a different aspect of the biographer's challenge while at the same time producing an original piece of writing. The "Snapshot Approach" (Chapter 4) introduces children to the biographer's need for a theme or design for organizing his or her material. "Fictionalized Versions" (Chapter 5) focuses attention on the narrative point of view and how it affects the content of a biography. It also allows writers the opportunity to create plausible events. "An Alternative to Chronological Order" (Chapter 6) shows children how to deviate from strict time order. "The Relationship between Life and Times" (Chapter 7) encourages children to explore how history and personality are related.

The chapters devoted to these strategies explain (1) the rationale of the approach, (2) the steps to follow, and (3) ways to enrich or extend the experience. Each strategy was tried at least once in an intermediate-grade classroom, and details of these experiences are provided.

The four strategies are presented in the approximate order of their difficulty. However, it is not necessary to use them in this order. They are meant, instead, to help children explore different aspects of biography.

II. Biography in the Classroom: Approaches for Beginners

4 The Snapshot Approach

The major challenge biographers face is bringing order to the mass of data they collect. As they read, take notes, reflect, and do all the various things researchers do, they are looking for ways to shape their material. Whether they call it themes, threads, keys, groups, or principles, it all boils down to the same thing. Biographers are always searching for a way to give coherence to what at first seems like a collection of separate items. They are hoping to suddenly discover a design that makes it all fit together.

The purpose of the Snapshot Approach is to give children the experience of bringing order or coherence to data the way a professional biographer does. Using this approach, children search for common themes or threads within the material they have researched. They discover their own designs that give shape to a life story. They find their own unique way of understanding their subject.

The Snapshot Approach makes use of children's ability to visualize memorable events in the life of the person being studied (Zarnowski 1986). These "snapshots," or pictures formed in the mind's eye, become the basis for many of the other steps in the process of organizing material—steps involving speaking, drawing, and writing. A snapshot, first pictured in the mind and then drawn and written about, corresponds to information the biographer selects as memorable enough to include.

The biographer's overall design shows how all the material in a biography fits together. It gives the work unity. Like professional biographers, children who write biography discover designs that are quite original. For example, several fifth graders who wrote a snapshot biography of Eleanor Roosevelt organized their writing by contrasting the painful and unpleasant experiences in Mrs. Roosevelt's early life with the exciting and unique experiences in her later life. This design gave shape to a large portion of the data they uncovered during their research (Zarnowski 1988).

The Snapshot Approach consists of four steps which lead students to first select material and then discover a design for a biography. These steps are (1) learning about the subject, (2) brainstorming and selecting material, (3) preparing the snapshots, and (4) arranging the material and discovering a design. Each of these steps is explained in more detail below. Along with the description is an account of what happened when Lila Alexander and I tried this approach with the students in her fifth-grade class in a New York City public school.

Steps to Follow

Teacher Preparation

Before beginning the project, some teacher preparation is required. First, the teacher must select the subject the class will research and write about. Second, a selection of biographies and related materials must be gathered. There must be enough material to accommodate an entire class.

When Ms. Alexander and I planned our project, we selected Eleanor Roosevelt as our subject. Chief among our reasons was an interest in introducing more women's history into the curriculum. In addition, we took a trip to the local library where we found a large number of children's biographies of Mrs. Roosevelt and a great deal of primary source material. Finding appropriate reading material was an important consideration for us, since we planned to buy very few books. Instead, we combed several neighborhood libraries and were able to put together quite a substantial collection. A number of students also helped us gather books from libraries and from their homes. Once the material was gathered, we were ready for step 1.

Step 1: Learning about the Subject

During the first step, children learn as much as possible about the subject. Every day for approximately one month, the class reads, listens, asks questions, and tracks down information. They begin by listening to the teacher read aloud for approximately twenty minutes each day from a biography of the subject. This book should have a lively style and be relatively short. Listening to a book read aloud provides the children with important background that they can draw on later when they begin to read independently. During the first week or two, after each day's reading, the teacher writes down the responses of the group, noting what the children think is important enough to remember and their feelings about this information (see "Writing Group Responses" in Chapter 3). The teacher is modeling what the children will later be doing by themselves when they write in their journals.

Once the book is finished, maybe a week or two later, a number of procedural changes take place. The children now have sufficient background information to begin reading about the subject independently and writing responses in their journals. The teacher's role changes, too. Instead of reading biographies aloud, the teacher begins to introduce primary source material. This material can be a letter written by the subject, a newspaper article, a photograph, or a significant quote. Because of the reading and listening that has gone before, children can appreciate this material. They have built up a context for understanding it.

The ideal amount of time to devote to this step is an hour a day for approximately one month. Twenty minutes is usually set aside for listening to the teacher read aloud from a biography or share primary source materials, another twenty minutes for silent reading, and ten minutes for journal writing. Of course, other variations are possible. Sometimes there is only time for listening to the teacher read or for reading independently and jotting down responses in a journal. These two activities can alternate—listening one day, reading and journal-writing the next.

In Ms. Alexander's class, daily periods of forty-five minutes to an hour were set aside for the study of Eleanor Roosevelt. To begin, Ms. Alexander read aloud Doris Faber's *Eleanor Roosevelt: First Lady of the World*. This well-written book captured the children's interest and engaged their sympathies. It was also short. At less than sixty pages, it provided a brief overview that children could later supplement through their own research. And since Faber's book is available as a paperback, we were able to afford a few copies for the classroom library.

Once the book was completed, Ms. Alexander read excerpts from a biography written by Mrs. Roosevelt's son Elliott, followed by portions of Mrs. Roosevelt's autobiography. At other times she shared pictures, magazine and newspaper articles, films and pamphlets. One child even brought in a story written by Eleanor Roosevelt that his mother had found in a magazine. As a result of their daily listening, reading, and writing, the children were becoming quite knowledgeable. They felt as if they were authorities on the life of Eleanor Roosevelt. In fact, a number of parents commented to both Ms. Alexander and me that their children were frequently talking about Mrs. Roosevelt at home.

Towards the end of the first month of this project, I carefully examined the children's journals. I found that from the start there was evidence that the children were developing their own sympathetic friendships with Mrs. Roosevelt. These friendships were based partly on feelings of admiration and partly on feelings of sympathy and empathy. In addition to this, a number of children were beginning to create their own designs. This took the form of general statements supported by a

Type of Response	Journal Example
Admiration	Eleanor gave much of her time to make this a much better world for all people. I am very proud of her. I would also give my life away to help the poor and the ones who need help still.
	I read about a wise and gracious lady.
Sympathy/ Empathy	I feel sorry for her that she is so ugly, but I really wish I was her. She had a good heart, but was ugly.
	I felt sad for her because she had no mother. Her father was [in] N.Y. She had to stay with Grandma Hall.
	I feel real happy for Eleanor Roosevelt because she really loves him [her father] and he loves her. They really get to see each other. That means a lot to her and that is why I feel real happy for her.
	I feel very happy for her because she finally got married and had a baby.
Generalization and Details (Themes beginning to emerge)	*Eleanor Roosevelt's childhood was not a happy one.* And parties were always a time of special agony for her because she was so shy. She knew she was not beautiful. And she knew she was the first girl in her family not to be a belle. [italics added]
	. *Eleanor was a very busy person.* She traveled almost all over the world. She became interested in very important business. She felt like F.D.R.'s investigator. . . . She visited hospitals during World War II. [italics added]

Figure 5. Journal entries written about Eleanor Roosevelt.

number of supporting details. Figure 5 shows a sampling of the kinds of comments I found in the journals.

On the basis of our classroom observations and our examination of the children's journals, Ms. Alexander and I agreed that the children were ready to move on to step 2—selecting material for their biographies.

Step 2: Brainstorming and Selecting Material

As children become knowledgeable about their subject *and* as their journals show that they have developed some emotional attachment, it

- When Eleanor went to the French boarding school she felt out of place because everyone was french.
- Eleanor lied to get attention, just a story
- At Eleanor's wedding, her + her groom were not payed attention to, instead her uncle Teddy Roosevelt took the floor.
- As a young girl the only friend Eleanor had except her father, of course was their butler, Victor.
- Eleanor was related to Franklin she was married.
- On March 4th 1933, Eleanor became lady of the land."
- After Franklin's death Eleanor did not get remarried.
- Eleanor's uncle taught her how to ride a horse.
- Eleanor had five children.
- Eleanor named her baby after her father, Eliott.
- Eleanor's speeches were about the Depression + War

Figure 6. A list of remembered events.

is time for them to gather and select the material that will actually appear in the biography. To do this, children are divided into groups of four to six students. The goal of each group is to brainstorm a list of all the events they can remember that happened in the subject's life.

During the brainstorming session, one student in each group serves as a secretary while the rest of the group contributes to the list. No one should be concerned about writing things down in chronological order. The emphasis is on remembering and gathering what is recalled.

Once the list is compiled, students examine it carefully and select the five to ten events they consider to be the most important events in the subject's life. These events will later be made into "snapshots" which will form the basis of the resulting biography.

In Ms. Alexander's class, brainstorming and the selection of material were completed during two class sessions. The brainstorming was completed during the first session. Before the groups began working by themselves, one group was asked to demonstrate the process for the entire class. Then, when everyone was clear about what to do, the groups were allowed to function on their own.

Although the children's first impulse was to reach for their books and journals to help them make their lists of important events, we advised them to rely only on what they could recall as being truly memorable. We were not certain what the results would be, but after forty-five minutes of conversation each group had a list. The shortest was two pages and the longest was five. We found these lists truly impressive.

During the second session the groups used their lists to select the events they wanted to write about. Several topics emerged in almost every group: Eleanor's early home life, her school experiences, her marriage, FDR's paralysis, and her political career. These would become important "threads" in the designs of many of the final biographies. Figure 6 shows a portion of one group's brainstorming list and three of the events they selected.

Step 3: Preparing the Snapshots

After the brainstorming session, the groups continue to work together. Each group member chooses one or more of the selected events to make into a snapshot.

A snapshot consists of a picture of an event and a written description. First, the children are asked to visualize the event, to close their eyes and picture it, and then to draw it. Their drawings should contain as much detail as possible. After drawing, the children write about their pictures, telling what is happening. Detail is valued here, too, since this writing becomes the text of the biography.

Ms. Alexander's students produced snapshots that were a mixture of fact and interpretation. For example, in a snapshot of Eleanor's experience at a French boarding school, the writer speculates about Eleanor's feelings of loneliness and confusion (see Figure 7). Likewise, a snapshot of Eleanor's wedding reveals more about the writer's anger than about Eleanor's (see Figure 8). When the bride and groom were upstaged by Uncle Teddy, they took the experience in stride. Eleanor reportedly found it amusing.

How Eleanor Felt About Her New School

Eleanor Roosevelt felt left out, first of all, because her parents wanted her out of the way when her mother had a baby. They sent her to school where she didn't know the language. It must have been very hard for her to relate with the people and it must have been harder for her to understand the other children. She must have been very lonely without seeing her father very often. He was important to her because he understood her more than anybody. I think for a little girl her age she must have been lonely. She did not have any idea why her parents were sending her to a school where she didn't understand the language.

Figure 7. Snapshot of Eleanor's experience at boarding school.

To produce the final snapshots, the children in Ms. Alexander's class made several sketches and more than one written draft. There was the usual work of selecting material to include, adding details, omitting unnecessary information, getting feedback from friends, editing, and finally recopying. When the snapshots were completed, each group received a large piece of posterboard for displaying their work. The students were then ready for the final step of the project.

When Eleanor and Franklin Got Married

Eleanor got married to her fifth cousin when she was nineteen. They got married in the White House. At first Eleanor didn't want to get married in the White House because it was too big and too popular. When Eleanor and Franklin got married, most of the people were looking at Teddy Roosevelt because he was president. Eleanor was angry because everyone was looking at Teddy Roosevelt.

Figure 8. Snapshot of Eleanor's wedding.

Step 4: Arranging the Material and Discovering a Design

Each group arranges all the completed snapshots in chronological order going clockwise, either pasted on large posterboard or tacked onto a bulletin board so that they can be seen by the entire group. Figure 9 shows the form for arranging a snapshot biography.

Next the group prepares a summary statement based on their snapshots. As the group examines all of the snapshots they produced, they consider the following questions: In what ways are the events shown in the snapshots similar? In general, how would you describe the subject's life? The summary statement is composed jointly by the members of the group. It should bring together the common threads the children have found in the snapshots and correspond to the biographer's search for coherence.

One of the summary statements made by a group of Ms. Alexander's students contrasted Eleanor's early life with her later years. The group found that, in spite of what they considered her "tragic childhood," in her later years she led an "exciting life" as First Lady and delegate to the United Nations. They wrote:

Eleanor's Tragic Life and Exciting Life

Eleanor had a tragic childhood. Eleanor Roosevelt was only eight years old when her mother died. Her father was an alcoholic. He was the only person Eleanor liked. Eleanor had to go live with her grandmother. . . .

When she was grown up she had an exciting life. Everyone gave Eleanor alot of attention. She finally got a man she loved, her fifth cousin Franklin Roosevelt. He became president and she was First Lady. She later joined the U.N.

In this dramatic turnabout, the children seemed to find hope. An unhappy childhood does not necessarily lead to an unhappy and unproductive adulthood. This contrast also provided a framework for understanding and organizing the events of Mrs. Roosevelt's life.

Looking Back at the Snapshot Approach

Of the four strategies described in this book, the Snapshot Approach is the easiest to implement. This plan provides each child with a great deal of support through group interaction and decision making. The writing required, too, is divided up among the group members. In effect, four or five students complete one biography.

Yet, despite the simplicity and ease of this project, it provides a meaningful introduction to the major challenge of writing biography. The

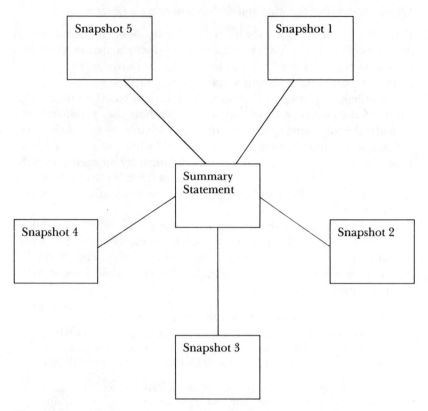

Figure 9. Form for arranging a snapshot biography.

lessons children learn about coherence and design are relevant to anyone who reads or writes biography.

Going Further

The Snapshot Approach to biography can be extended, modified, and reused. Here are a few ideas for related projects.

1. The same format can be used to make a snapshot autobiography. Children can write about their own lives, using photographs as well as drawings. They can interview their parents, relatives, and acquaintances for information and consult documents related to their own lives, such as their birth certificates, report cards, and awards from school or clubs.

2. Snapshot biographies can be written about living subjects who are available for interview. These subjects can be people the children know well, such as friends, classmates, teachers, and relatives, or they can be local residents with careers or experiences the children find interesting.

3. Students can make oral presentations based on their snapshot biographies. The content of the biography provides the speaker with information and thoughts to share. The illustrations, which can be referred to during the presentation, help the speaker stick to the topic. Various groups completing a snapshot biography can make presentations to each other. Even if the groups have studied the same subject, they can look for similarities and differences between the biographies.

4. The events described in a snapshot biography can be dramatized. Each snapshot becomes a scene in a play. A narrator can introduce the play and provide background information for the various scenes. Students can improvise the dialogue or write it down. If the dialogue is written down, it can be tape-recorded and placed in a listening center.

In this chapter, the approach to biography is through the use of authentic materials. The next chapter describes the use of fictionalized accounts as a model for writing biography. The writing that results is highly imaginative since writers are asked to speculate about *what might have happened.*

5 Fictionalized Versions

Fictionalized biographies, a mixture of fiction and nonfiction, give the writer the opportunity to create something that history has not supplied. That "something" can be conversations that *might have taken place*, events that *might have occurred*, or details that a keen observer *might have noticed*. The writer tries to provide plausible answers to some of history's unanswered questions.

Authors of fictionalized biographies are not free to let their imaginations run wild. Instead, they create what they believe is likely to have happened. They fill in gaps in the evidence that is currently available. The resulting work contains a great deal more fact than fiction.

This approach is an appealing one for young writers because it lets them tie up loose ends and flesh out a story that would otherwise have gaps in it. Filling in these gaps makes the story more complete and more satisfying. It answers, at least for the moment, the questions children want answered.

For example, two youngsters writing about Ben Franklin examined the complex relationship he had with his brother James. They tried to put themselves in James's shoes and see Ben's actions from his point of view. As a result, they concluded that James both resented and admired his younger brother. On the one hand, James resented Ben's failure to honor the terms of his apprenticeship. Assuming James's point of view, they wrote:

> When he came to work for me, we made an agreement. His part of the bargain was to be loyal to me, keep my secrets, and work for me until he was 21. I kept my part of the bargain but Ben didn't.

On the other hand, since they also concluded that James admired his brother, they added:

> Ben did a lot of things. He wrote Poor Richard's Almanac, helped write the peace treaty between the United States and England, and much later he signed the Constitution. Despite how poorly we got along, I was PROUD! of my little brother for all of those things.

The process of writing fictionalized biography requires children to think about the information they are learning in order to build upon it.

The approach invites children to imagine, to speculate, and to suggest ideas. In this way, thinking, learning, and writing go hand in hand.

Steps to Follow

The approach to writing fictionalized biographies consists of three steps: (1) listening to fictionalized biographies read aloud by the teacher, (2) learning about the subject of the biography, and (3) planning and writing the fictionalized biographies. These steps are explained below. Along with this explanation is a description of my experience in Mildred Sturman's fourth-grade class, when she and her students wrote fictionalized biographies of Benjamin Franklin.

Step 1: Listening to Fictionalized Biographies

In order to write fictionalized biographies, children must be familiar with them. The biographies of F. N. Monjo provide a good introduction because of their consistent use of the same fictional techniques.

Five of Monjo's books, which he refers to as his "shirt-sleeve miniatures" (1975, 435), follow a format children can use in their own writing. Each book is a portrait of a famous American statesman narrated by a son, grandson, or granddaughter. Monjo specifically chose to use a child as narrator in order to limit the content of the biography to just those things a child would understand and consider important. A child narrator enabled him to omit events he believed were beyond a child's comprehension or would be of limited interest.

Monjo uses the child-as-narrator approach very successfully. In his biography of Theodore Roosevelt, *The One Bad Thing about Father*, Quentin Roosevelt, Theodore's son, tells a great deal about living in the White House and playing with his father, while only briefly mentioning that his father mediated the end of the Russo-Japanese War. Similarly, in *Grand Papa and Ellen Aroon*, Thomas Jefferson's granddaughter tells more about Jefferson's role as a loving grandfather than about his role in writing the Declaration of Independence. In this way, Monjo avoids overpacking his biographies with more facts than young readers want to know.

Yet, in spite of the fictionalized scenes and dialogue, Monjo's biographies are "about ninety-eight percent fact" (Monjo 1975, 439). At the end of each book, the author points out the parts he created, enabling the reader to distinguish between fact and fiction. He tells us, for instance, that Quentin Roosevelt and Ellen Aroon never really told stories about their famous relatives. Instead, these stories are written the way they *might have told* them.

The following books are referred to as the "shirt-sleeve miniatures":

1. *Grand Papa and Ellen Aroon: Being an Account of Some of the Happy Times Spent Together by Thomas Jefferson and His Favorite Granddaughter* (illustrated by Richard Cuffari), Holt, Rinehart and Winston, 1974.

2. *Me and Willie and Pa: The Story of Abraham Lincoln and His Son Tad* (illustrated by D. Gorsline), Simon and Schuster, 1973.

3. *The One Bad Thing about Father* (illustrated by Rocco Negri), Harper and Row, 1970.

4. *Poor Richard in France* (illustrated by Brinton Turkle), Holt, Rinehart and Winston, 1973.

5. *The Vicksburg Veteran* (illustrated by Douglas Gorsline), Simon and Schuster, 1971.

To begin the project in fictionalized biography, children listen as their teacher reads each of these biographies aloud. Some are short enough to be read in one sitting, while others require two or three class sessions.

After each biography is read, a data chart like the one shown in Figure 10 is filled in by the teacher and the students together. The chart helps the children generalize about the recurring features of Monjo's biographies. By focusing on the narrator, the subject, and the content of each book, it eventually becomes apparent that (1) the narrator is always a child who knows the subject, (2) the subject is always a famous American, and (3) the content is always about the subject's habits and achievements. These are features that the children will later use when they write their own biographies.

Figure 10 is a portion of a larger chart completed by Ms. Sturman's fourth-grade class. Learning about fictionalized biographies took this class approximately one month. By the end of the month, the format of Monjo's biographies had become highly predictable. The children expected to hear about the life of a famous person told from the point of view of a child.

Step 2: Learning about the Subject of the Biography

Just as in the Snapshot Approach described in Chapter 4, this step involves the in-depth study of one person's life for a period of approximately one month. During this time, children engage in a number of activities in order to gather material.

Book Title	Famous Person the Story Is About	Person Telling the Story	Things the Person Has Done
Grand Papa and Ellen Aroon	Thomas Jefferson	Ellen Wayles Randolph, his granddaughter	1. He was the president. 2. He was called Mr. Mammoth. 3. He was a natural historian. 4. He loved to read. 5. He designed Monticello. 6. He wrote the Declaration of Independence. 7. He cut out poems and sent them to his grandchildren. 8. He introduced ice cream to this country.
The One Bad Thing about Father	Teddy Roosevelt, President (**T.R.**)	Quentin Roosevelt, his son	1. He stopped a war. 2. He always had time for his children. 3. He won the Nobel Prize. 4. He read poems to his children.
Poor Richard in France	Benjamin Franklin	Benjamin Franklin Bache, his grandson	1. He discovered that lightning and electricity are the same thing. 2. He invented the lightning rod. 3. He was a famous printer. 4. He took air baths. 5. He went to France to get help in the war.

Figure 10. Learning about F. N. Monjo's fictionalized biographies.

In the beginning, children listen as the teacher reads aloud each day from a biography of the subject or shares some primary source materials. After listening to one full-length biography and several original documents, the children are ready to begin reading about the subject independently and writing their responses in journals.

A typical one-hour schedule devoted to this project might be organized like this:

20 minutes—oral reading/discussion led by the teacher

30 minutes—silent reading

10 minutes—journal-writing

When Ms. Sturman's class began this step, she directed their attention to the study of Benjamin Franklin, the subject they would be writing about. Each day, she read aloud from a biography of Franklin. Her reading provided the students with background information about Franklin's character, his inventions, and the times in which he lived. This information helped them when they later began reading biographies on their own. As she discussed this material with her students, Ms. Sturman aroused their curiosity and motivated them to want to know more. How did Franklin manage to invent so many things? What were the particular circumstances?

As the students each began keeping journals, they were told to write down the information they wanted to remember *and* their feelings about that information. The resulting journal entries show that the students were reading for meaning and interpreting what they read. They didn't just pull out facts; they filtered the information they read through their minds and responded in a variety of ways. Some showed amusement:

> When he [Franklin] wrote a poem on the capture of Blackbeard and he asks his father's opinion and his father says you better stick to prose that was funny.

Others showed surprise:

> Ben lived in a small town. Ben was a little boy back in the 17 hundreds. The fact that they didn't have any addresses it was hard to find a person's house I bet. Thank god we have addresses. Just think walking around town looking for something that will tell you where the place is you're looking for.

A few reported feelings of confusion:

> I read about the American Revolution. I did not like this part because I did not understand it.

And many recorded their feelings of empathy and friendship:

> His [Franklin's] first day at school. I was happy when he was happy. I think he was the best student in the class.

After spending one month learning about Ben Franklin, Ms. Sturman and I were convinced that the students were quite knowledgeable about the events in his life. We decided to make the transition from reading about Franklin to writing fictionalized biographies about him.

Step 3: Planning and Writing the Fictionalized Biographies

Once children have learned about fictionalized biographies and about their subject (steps 1 and 2), they are ready to put that knowledge to work. As they begin to write their own fictionalized biographies, the teacher provides the supports that make this task possible. These supports consist of explanations, demonstrations, and trial runs.

One important explanation the teacher provides is telling children about planning. A planning sheet like the one shown in Figure 11 helps children make important decisions before they begin to write. This sheet focuses children's attention on those aspects of fictionalized biography that need to be decided: (1) the narrator, (2) the story, and (3) the facts included in the story. Once these decisions are made, the writer has a direction to follow. Although this direction may change during the process of writing and rethinking, it is enough to get a writer started.

One way to use this planning sheet is for teachers to think through their own fictionalized biographies and share their decision making with the class. The teacher's planning sheet can be prepared ahead of time or right in front of the children. A draft based on this planning sheet can also be shared. As the teacher demonstrates and discusses his or her decision-making process, the children are "let in" on the procedure. The teacher is demonstrating and explaining how a fictionalized biography is written.

Another use for this planning sheet is for trial runs, when the teacher and the class plan a fictionalized biography together and begin to write

---

1. Who could tell a story about Benjamin Franklin?

2. What will the story be about? What happens?

3. What "facts" will you include?

Figure 11. Planning sheet for writing a fictionalized biography.

1. Who could tell a story about Benjamin Franklin?

   Jonathan, a Leather Apron member

2. What will the story be about? What happens?

   Jonathan tells how Ben helped the public.

3. What "facts" will you include?
   a. retired from business in 1748
   b. spent time on public service projects
   c. formed Leather Apron Club to discuss important topics and try to improve life in Philadelphia
   d. Leather Apron Club later called Junto Club
   e. with members of the Junto Club made plans for lighting the city of Philadelphia
   f. was one of the founders of the first public library
   g. organized first volunteer fire department
   h. raised money for the first hospital in Philadelphia

Figure 12. Planning sheet completed with the class.

a story. This demonstrates the procedures to follow and enables the children to participate by suggesting ideas for the story. If the teacher does the writing, the children are free to concentrate on generating ideas. Since the whole class works together, no one is responsible for making all the decisions.

A planning sheet completed during a trial run in Ms. Sturman's class is shown in Figure 12, and the opening paragraph for a story is shown in Figure 13.

After completing two trial runs on two different occasions, the children in Ms. Sturman's class began working on their own planning sheets and writing their own biographies. The class spent three weeks drafting, revising, and illustrating. During that time, there was a great deal of sharing with classmates and conferencing with the teacher. A final edited version of each biography was ultimately made into an illustrated book.

The opening paragraph of ten-year-old Flori's book shows how successfully she was able to combine what she had learned about Monjo's narrative technique with what she had learned about Ben Franklin:

> I am Benjamin Franklin's sister and I can tell you a few things about him. It all started January 17, 1706, with the birth of my brother Benjamin. He was the fifteenth of our father's and mother's seventeen children. One of the first events of a newborn baby's life is being carried in his father's arms. I was proud to show off my new baby brother.

The complete text of Flori's biography is included in Appendix A.

Ben Franklin, Public Servant

My name is Jonathan, and I'm telling about my friend Ben. He was a good friend. We were in the Leather Apron Club together. We tried to get things done like getting lights on the streets and keeping the streets clean.

Figure 13. Opening paragraph from a fictionalized biography based on the planning sheet.

Looking Back at Fictionalized Versions

Writing fictionalized biography teaches children about the powerful effect of the narrator. The way a narrator tells a story is determined by what he or she knows and considers important. This is true not only for Monjo's biographies with their child-narrators but for all biographies. To a large extent, biographies vary according to the concerns of the person telling the story.

Since this project makes use of both fictionalized and authentic biographical material, it broadens children's understanding of biography as a genre. Children are in a position to realize that there are different approaches to biography as well as considerable room for experimentation.

The negotiated balance between fact and fiction makes this approach an enjoyable one. Who doesn't enjoy telling stories about relatives, friends, and acquaintances—and by extension, historical figures—and embellishing them just a bit? The impulse to add a few "stretchers" is almost irresistible.

Going Further

A study of fictionalized biography can be extended and enriched in a number of ways:

1. Children can share and discuss the biographies they have written. How are biographies written from different points of view similar? How are they different?
2. Besides the titles already mentioned, F. N. Monjo has written several other books for children that are suitable for reading aloud or for independent reading. Two titles should be particularly interesting to children who are already familiar with Monjo's biographies. *King George's Head Was Made of Lead* is a "history" narrated by a statue of the king that was melted down to make Yankee bullets during the American Revolution. *Letters to Horseface* consists of letters Wolf-

gang Amadeus Mozart *might* have written to his sister during his trip to Italy.

3. Robert Lawson has written three entertaining fictionalized biographies using animals as narrators. *Ben and Me* is the story of Ben Franklin as told by a mouse named Amos; *Mr. Revere and I* is Paul Revere's story as told by his horse; and *Captain Kidd's Cat* is the infamous pirate's story as told by his loyal tabby. These books can be read and enjoyed and can also serve as models for writing biographies from the point of view of an animal.

4. Assuming the role of narrator, children can write fictionalized biographies of people they know well. The subject can be a parent, sibling, or friend.

Both the Snapshot Approach and Fictionalized Versions are based on time order. The next chapter considers an alternative to strict chronological order: beginning at the peak of a subject's career.

6 An Alternative to Chronological Order

Do biographers have to begin at the beginning and follow a birth-to-death sequence? Not necessarily. Leon Edel, biographer and literary critic, argues convincingly against the need for always following strict chronology. According to Edel (1984), the biographer should be free to use the same narrative techniques as the novelist, including flashbacks, flash-forwards, summaries, and retrospectives. Such techniques help writers develop the underlying themes and patterns they discover in their material. According to Edel, successful biographers "melt down" their material to reveal its essence. If not, they risk being buried in a mass of details.

The idea of beginning a biography at the peak of a person's career instead of at the moment of birth raises some interesting possibilities for classroom inquiries. It enables children to deal with some of their most pressing questions. These questions surfaced quite forcefully when Ms. Alexander's fifth-grade class studied the life of Eleanor Roosevelt. Many children commented on the sharp contrast between Roosevelt's childhood and her adulthood. Isn't it strange, they asked, that a painfully shy, submissive, and quiet girl grew into a vocal, active, and highly visible public figure? And, indeed it is. How did this metamorphosis happen? What are the roots of this change? What, if anything, prepared the shy, unassuming Eleanor to become the "First Lady of the World"?

Even after our study of Eleanor Roosevelt was completed, the same questions remained: Do the early events in a person's life serve as preparation for later adult roles? Or are there sometimes surprising and unexpected turnarounds between childhood and adulthood? These questions prompted me to follow Edel's lead and examine life histories in a different way.

The following year, Ms. Alexander and I took up these questions again with a different group of children who were pursuing an in-depth study of George Washington. First, the children considered Washington during one of the "high points" of his career—as either commander in chief or first president. Then they looked back at his earlier life. Was he prepared for these roles? Or, given his upbringing, was it surprising and unexpected that he later assumed these roles?

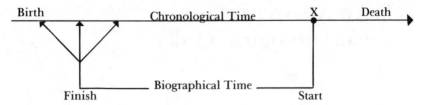

Figure 14. The direction of a nonchronological biography.

The strategy we used, An Alternative to Chronological Order, helped children write about Washington's career without being tied to a strict chronological sequence. In fact, as shown in Figure 14, this type of biography moves in the opposite direction of chronological time. The biography begins with a description of the subject at the height of his or her career and then looks backward for the roots of that career.

This strategy focuses children's attention on developing a position and backing it up with relevant information. The writer argues either that the subject *was* prepared or *was not* prepared for a later role. This is a more challenging task than producing a remembered chain of events in a person's life.

Steps to Follow

A nonchronological strategy suitable for beginning biographers consists of five steps: (1) learning about the subject, (2) developing a time line, (3) confronting the major question, (4) gathering relevant arguments, and (5) writing the biography. Each step is described in more detail below. Along with the description is an account of what happened when Ms. Alexander's fifth graders followed this plan.

Step 1: Learning about the Subject

As in the two approaches already discussed, this strategy begins with in-depth study. The class spends approximately one month completing the following activities: listening to the teacher read one or more biographies of the subject, sharing and discussing primary source material, reading several biographies independently, and writing responses to these biographies in their journals.

These basic procedures for in-depth study can also be enriched. For example, during the time that Ms. Alexander's class studied George Washington, in addition to the activities outlined above, they also decided to have a colonial-style luncheon. With the help of several cookbooks, the children were able to prepare a number of dishes served during Washington's time. This may have been inspired by a reading of Jean Fritz's book *George Washington's Breakfast*, a book that taught the children, among other things, what the general ate each morning.

Besides their colonial luncheon, the class completed a number of other related activities. After they listened to Ms. Alexander read Milton Meltzer's biography *George Washington and the Birth of Our Nation*, they invited the author for a morning of biographer-to-biographer conversation. The children also visited Fraunces Tavern, the site where Washington bid farewell to his troops. And, finally, they produced an amusing classroom display by copying and illustrating the rules of behavior that Washington wrote for himself in his own notebooks. Under one child's illustration was written the following rule: "In the presence of others, sing not to yourself with a humming noise, nor drum with your fingers or feet."

An in-depth study of the subject lays the foundation for the rest of the process and generates enthusiasm for the subject. Nothing can make up for the experience of being deeply immersed in a subject and having the time to explore it. This is the basis for building interesting ideas.

An intriguing example of student engagement with the life of George Washington occurred at the end of one student's journal. For weeks this student steadily reported each of the events she read about. Then towards the end of her journal there is an abrupt change from reporting to forming mental images. The student wrote:

> I see him in this chair doing his work.
> I see him upon a horse riding down the street smiling.

Images like these form the basis of interpretive thinking. In the student's final biography she used both of these images. At one point she included an illustration showing Washington at his desk. A caption reads, "George in his office thinking about if he should help the French." The accompanying text describes Washington's unpopular decision to ignore the French request for assistance in their war against the British. At another point the student described Washington out on a snowy day, riding his horse around Mount Vernon. In both of these instances, the writer used her images to develop a vivid portrait of Washington.

Step 2: Developing a Time Line

After the period of in-depth study, the class constructs a time line of major events in the subject's life. This can be completed by the whole class working together, or small groups can brainstorm together for

- 1799 Death

- 1789 Becomes first president
- 1787 Signs U.S. Constitution
- 1783 Peace treaty signed; British acknowledge American independence

- 1776 Revolutionary War
- 1775 Becomes commander in chief

- 1765 Britain imposes Stamp Act
- 1763 End of French and Indian War
- 1759 Marries Martha Custis
- 1756 French and Indian War begins
- 1754 Resigned from the militia
- 1751 Joined the army

- 1747 Became a surveyor

- 1743 His father died

- 1738 Moved up the Rappahannock

- 1732 Birth

Figure 15. A time line of remembered events in the life of George
          Washington.

remembered events and then bring their information back to the larger
group. One or two class periods should be sufficient for completing this
step.

The purpose of the time line is to identify what the class considers to
be the high points of the subject's career. One of these high points will
serve as the starting point for a nonchronological biography.

Figure 15 shows the time line developed by Ms. Alexander's class. As
a result of preparing this time line, the class decided that the high points
of Washington's career were (1) when he became commander in chief of
the American army and (2) when he became the first American president. This meant that students would begin their biographies with a
description of Washington in one of these two roles. In order to do this,
the class reviewed and discussed their understanding of what happened
during both of these phases of Washington's career.

Step 3: Confronting the Major Question

Once the starting point of the biography is selected, children are ready
to confront the major question: Was the subject prepared for his or her
important role? This is the question that children will be answering in
their biographies.

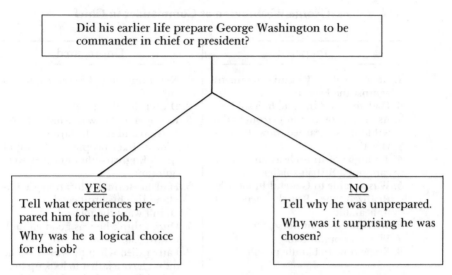

Figure 16. Comparing early life and later life. Confronting the major questions.

A diagram like the one used in Ms. Alexander's class (see Figure 16) frames the question clearly. The diagram focuses children's attention on first answering the question and then gathering arguments that support their position. It guides them as they attempt to take a stand.

Step 4: Gathering Relevant Arguments

Before writing their biographies, the children work together to gather relevant arguments for all the possible positions they can argue. As the material is gathered, it is compiled in charts which are displayed in the classroom. Later, as the children write, they are able to refer back to these charts.

In Ms. Alexander's class, students gathered arguments related to George Washington's career. Figure 17 shows arguments, pro and con, for Washington's preparedness as commander in chief. Figure 18 deals with his preparedness to be the first president.

The charts in Ms. Alexander's class grew rather large and contained much more material than any one child would incorporate into his or her biography. When many arguments had been collected—often twenty or more for a particular position—the children were in a power-ful position for determining their stances and "nailing down" their ideas.

George Washington as Commander in Chief

Prepared	Unprepared
1. At 21, led a Virginia regiment against the French.	1. Never trained to be commander in chief.
2. Had always wanted to be a soldier.	2. Didn't like the woods.
3. As a surveyor, he camped out in the wilderness—learned how to survive there.	3. Real goal in life was to be at Mount Vernon and run the farms.
4. Thought of himself as an American, not a British soldier.	4. Didn't like people who didn't speak English—thought they were ignorant.
5. Was an aide to General Braddock. Realized the British were not unbeatable.	5. Had no formal education in England like his brothers did.
6. Was an excellent horseman.	6. Didn't want the job.
7. Was very organized.	7. Didn't think he was good enough for the job.
8. Knew how to handle people.	8. Father died when he was 11, so he didn't have a father to look up to as a model and to help educate him.

Figure 17. Gathering relevant arguments: Washington as commander in chief.

Step 5: Writing the Biography

Using the diagram introduced during step 3 and the charts prepared during step 4, the children began to write their biographies. These biographies consisted of two parts: (1) a description of the subject at the high point of his or her career; (2) a comparison of early life and later life (Was he or she prepared?).

In my experience, writing the first part presented few problems for fifth-grade biographers. They plunged into their descriptions by immediately establishing the setting. For example, the opening paragraph of one student's biography immediately places Washington at the Second Continental Congress:

> On June 16, 1775 George Washington was in the Second Continental Congress. He was selected unanimously to be Commander in Chief. He thought it over. He thought it would be better if he were at Mount Vernon running his farm and being with his wife Martha and two step-children. He thought he was not good enough for [the] job. While he was thinking, he realized he had no choice. George took the job.

George Washington as President

Prepared	Unprepared
1. Had done a good job being in charge of Mount Vernon.	1. Was the first—had no models to follow.
2. Was very persuasive.	2. Didn't have a formal education.
3. Had experience organizing men.	3. Didn't want the job.
4. Was nice, honest, decent, determined, and courageous.	4. Was experienced leading people in war, not in peace.
5. Had served in the Virginia House of Burgesses.	5. Was embarrassed about being honored.
6. Learned love of freedom from the Fairfax family. Also learned that the most important thing a person could do was to serve his country.	6. Could not take criticism well—was short-tempered.
7. Had self-control: overcame his love for Sally Fairfax.	7. Had no practice. Said, "I walk on untrodden ground."
8. Didn't run away from his problems.	8. Didn't have much self-confidence—when young, women put him down.

Figure 18. Gathering relevant arguments: Washington as president.

It was while writing the second part, however, that students were challenged to reveal their most original thoughts. They prepared and shaped arguments that stemmed from their own ideas and interpretations. One fifth-grade biographer made the following interesting comparison about two of Washington's roles (italics added):

> He was also prepared [to be commander in chief] by taking care of Mount Vernon. He did many experiments with plants and animals that no one did. This may have given him the idea to experiment to plan new strategies. George had lots of land. He was very organized. *He organized his men like his crops, very carefully.*

Another student made this observation about Washington's suitability for the role of president (again, italics added):

> Though he didn't have a good education, he learned to love freedom from the Fairfax family. He also learned from them that the most important thing a person could do was serve his country. Those words helped George become mature and believe in himself. *It is important for a president to be mature and believe in himself because if he had to make a decision and the people didn't like it, he would have to believe that he made a right decision.*

Appendix B contains the complete texts of two nonchronological biographies of George Washington written by fifth-grade students. One deals with Washington as commander in chief, and the other deals with his career as the first president.

Looking Back at "An Alternative to Chronological Order"

The strategy developed in this chapter enlarges children's understanding of nonfiction literature by introducing them to yet another format for writing biography. According to James L. Clifford (1970), there are five major formats for biography. These vary along a continuum from the most objective to the most subjective. A format like the one discussed here most closely resembles the middle ground which Clifford refers to as the "artistic-scholarly" type of biography. Because an artistic-scholarly biography is midway between the most objective and the most subjective works, the writer of such a biography is free to arrange material as creatively as possible but is not allowed to invent episodes.

Chief among the practitioners of this type of biography is Leon Edel. His five-volume biography of Henry James uses every known way of manipulating time for the purpose of achieving an artistic result. While children are not ready to deal with Edel's complex work, they are ready to deal with the challenging idea behind it: that there are other ways besides chronology for organizing a biography. The strategy outlined in this chapter helps children to confront this idea.

Going Further

A study of alternatives to chronological order can be extended by looking at the various ways writers handle time and by experimenting with some of those ways.

1. Children can examine the opening chapters of several biographies. After examining biographies that start at the very beginning of a subject's life and biographies that do not, children can discuss which type of organization they find most appealing.

2. Some children might enjoy writing an autobiography that starts with a description of themselves in the present and then fills in their past. Other children might write nonchronological biographies of people they are acquainted with and can interview.

3. "You are there!" skits bring the past to life. After completing some background research and planning, a group of children can re-create a scene from the past.

4. A number of interesting stories have been written using a modern-day character who "falls into" a historical situation. Students might try traveling back in time and putting themselves into a historical setting. (For a listing of recommended time fantasies that draw children into different historical time periods, see Huck, Hepler, and Hickman 1987, 368–69, and Cullinan 1989, 299–303.)

The strategy discussed in this chapter helps students to confront the issue of time when writing a biography. The next chapter also deals with time but focuses students' attention on the relationship between a subject's life and times.

7 The Relationship between Life and Times

Can a person make an impact on his or her times? Or do "the times" inevitably shape the person?

These questions yield no easy answers. Historians and biographers still ponder them. Some, like historian Arthur Schlesinger, Jr., (1988) claim that individuals can and *do* make an impact on society. At the same time, historians claim that the reason for this impact is the person's ability to respond to the currents and pressures of the times. A chicken-and-egg situation? Perhaps.

It is challenging to try to sort out and understand the relationship between a person's life and times. The process allows for meaningful, interesting dialogue. Like other truly provocative questions raised by the study of children's literature, this question is relevant for both children and adults (Matthews 1988).

Can children rise to the challenge? Absolutely. A fourth grader who was writing a biography of the life and times of Martin Luther King was asked to respond to the following questions: How did history affect Martin Luther King? How did Martin Luther King affect history? Here is what she wrote:

> How did history affect Martin? Well, when he was young, the Jim Crow laws started affecting him by not letting him play with his white friends, and not letting him go to the same schools as the white children did, and not letting him go to the same amusement parks as the white children did. This was hard on Martin.
>
> As he got a little older, history started affecting him more. Martin started leading non-violent marches like the Children's Crusade and March on Washington in 1963, and the Selma to Montgomery March in 1965. Martin was involved with so many things—like being elected president of the S.C.L.C. (Southern Christian Leadership Conference). He was being trusted to help the world.
>
> Martin made speeches that affected history. As he spoke, people understood more clearly what Martin had meant about segregation. . . . People started understanding how the black people felt. Every time the white people heard these speeches it gave them a bad feeling that what they had done was wrong.

In the space of three paragraphs this young author shows us the impact of segregation on Dr. King and his impact on the nation's social conscience.

The strategy described in this chapter encourages children to consider the interaction between a subject's life and times. In order to do this, a class focuses not only on the life of the subject, but also on events in history that occurred while the subject was alive. This historical background provides a context for understanding the events in the subject's life.

Steps to Follow

Writing a life-and-times biography consists of the following steps: (1) learning about the subject, (2) completing a time line, (3) brainstorming for topics to write about, and (4) preparing to write. Each of these steps is explained below in more detail, along with a description of my experience in Mildred Sturman's classroom when her fourth graders wrote life-and-times biographies of Dr. Martin Luther King, Jr.

Step 1: Learning about the Subject

This strategy, like the others described in this book, depends on in-depth learning about one particular subject. Children spend an hour a day for approximately one month learning about their subject. During this time, the teacher reads to them from a selected biography and shares primary source material. The children, in turn, read independently, keep journals, and share their responses with each other.

When Ms. Sturman and I selected the subject of our life-and-times biography project, we were looking for someone who had been "caught up" in his or her times. That subject could have been involved in politics, industry, education, science, or the arts. Our decision to select Dr. Martin Luther King rested to a large extent on his extraordinary involvement in the civil rights movement.

Dr. King proved to be an excellent choice because we found a wealth of material about him, including numerous biographies, films, and filmstrips. Copies of his speeches and letters were also readily available.

But what proved to be most exciting were the guests who came to Ms. Sturman's class to talk to the children about Dr. King. A Queens College student, a black woman, shared with the children a tape-recorded interview with her father, during which he discussed his memories of Dr. King. A Queens College professor of social studies education, a man who has traveled extensively in the South, told about his observations of the Jim Crow laws in action. And Ms. Sturman shared her own memories of the 1963 march on Washington. Seeing photographs and films of Dr. King and hearing people talk about their memories of him motivated the children to want to learn more about their subject.

At the end of one month, when I carefully examined the students' journals, I found that they had developed strong feelings of sympathy for Dr. King. One youngster wrote*:

> King got shot . . . in Memphis in 1968 at 6:00. Everybody was unhappy. *I feel as if my own relative has died.*

In addition, the children's journals abounded in angry denunciations of segregation and discrimination:

> King wanted the ballot, and so did some other black people. I didn't know that blacks couldn't vote like other people, so *I think it's unright.*

> After school he [King] ran to his friend's house. His [friend's] mother said M. L. and his friend couldn't play together because he was colored. *I felt it was a shock to M. L. and me.*

> M. L. went to a shoe store and Rev. King and M. L. had to sit in the back. *I think they should be treated the same as the whites.*

These feelings of anger at the unfair treatment Dr. King endured caused the children to become his champions. They suffered his defeats and shared his triumphs. They were eager to learn how he dealt with injustices.

While the issue of fairness raged within Ms. Sturman's fourth-grade class, other issues can serve just as well to motivate children's reading. As noted in previous chapters, children have responded to Eleanor Roosevelt's unhappy childhood and the sibling rivalry between Benjamin Franklin and his brother. Emotional issues such as these appeal to children's desire to know how people deal with conflict. This desire to know sustains children's interest in books.

Step 2: Completing a Time Line

As children continue their research, they can also begin working on a time line spanning the years of the subject's life. A format like the one shown in Figure 19 provides space for recording events in the subject's life as well as related events in history.

The purpose of this time line is to help children *see* when historic events occurred in relation to events in the subject's life. Writing down this information makes it available for analysis and discussion. The

---

*Here and throughout the chapter, italics in students' work have been added.

Events in the Subject's Life		Events in History
	1900	
	1901	
	1902	
	1903	
	1904	
	1905	
	1906	
	1907	
	1908	

Figure 19. A time line format for a life-and-times biography.

information becomes quite useful when the children begin to plan and write their biographies because they do not have to rely on memory.

Everyone in Ms. Sturman's class worked on the time line together. Ms. Sturman used a large bulletin board and made her time line large enough for the class to read. The children received paper copies to complete and keep for their own use.

After each day's research, the class added to their time lines. Once the time lines were finished, the children were able to see both the personal events in King's life (e.g., the birth of his daughter Yolanda) and his growing involvement in the civil rights movement (e.g., his leadership of the Southern Christian Leadership Conference). Figure 20 shows a portion of our class time line. Notice that we limited the scope of history

Events in King's Life		Events in History (Civil Rights)
Graduated Boston University	1955	Rosa Parks arrested
Went to Dexter Ave. Church,		Montgomery Improvement Asso-
Montgomery		ciation formed
Yolanda born		Bus boycott begins
	1956	SCLC formed; MLK president
		Supreme Court outlaws bus segre-
		gation
MLK leads SCLC	1957	
Becomes full-time pastor of Dexter		
Ave. Church		
Stabbed		
	1958	
	1959	
Resigns as pastor and moves to	1960	"Sit-ins" begin
Atlanta		JFK running for president
Becomes assistant pastor in		Protest marches organized all over
father's church		South
Arrested at "sit-in" and jailed		
	1961	
	1962	
MLK and Ralph Abernathy lead	1963	Birmingham March (Children's
Children's March/Gives "I have a		Crusade)
dream" speech during Washington		March on Washington
March		President Kennedy assassinated

Figure 20. The life and times of Martin Luther King: A portion of the time line.

to include only events related to the civil rights movement. These would be the events most likely to make an impact on King's life.

When the time lines were completed, most children had read between five and ten books about Dr. King and had discussed his life extensively.

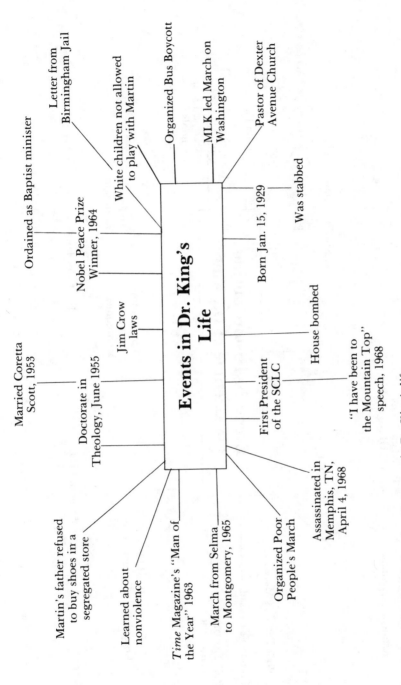

Figure 21. A web showing the events in Dr. King's life.

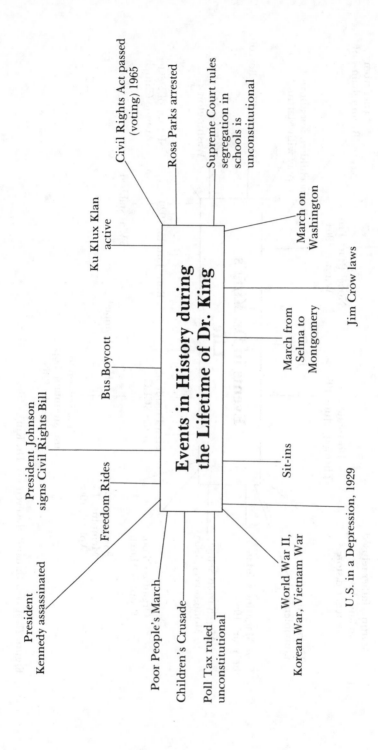

Figure 22. A web showing events in history.

They were ready for the next step, making decisions about the content of their biographies.

Step 3: Brainstorming for Topics to Write About

Based on their accumulated knowledge, at this point children are ready to select the topics they will write about in their biographies. Selection implies that the material to be included is important to the biographer's understanding of the subject. It is significant.

Without making the decisions for them, the teacher provides the students with a process for deciding what to include. This process consists of (1) brainstorming in small groups in order to form two lists of remembered events and (2) selecting from these lists the events that the class will later write about in their biographies.

Ms. Sturman's class held two brainstorming sessions. During the first session, the children listed all the events in Martin Luther King's life that they could remember. They were asked to respond to the following questions: What happened to Martin Luther King during his lifetime? What did he *do* during his lifetime?

During the second brainstorming session, the class made a list of historical events that occurred during King's lifetime. They responded to this question: What was happening in the U.S. during Martin Luther King's life?

Figures 21 and 22 show the "life" and "time" webs produced by the children and Ms. Sturman when they pooled the various group lists. Ms. Sturman printed the final webs on large poster boards and hung them on the wall so that the class could use them later when they selected the actual events they would write about.

Step 4: Preparing to Write

The webs will contain more events than most beginning writers can comfortably incorporate in their biographies. In order to make their writing manageable, they can select from their webs those events to include and those to omit. This means weighing the significance of all the events.

The selected events are organized according to the following chapter outline:

Chapter I: The Times

Chapter II: The Life

Chapter III: The Life and Times

When Ms. Sturman's class was ready to plan the content of their biographies, they referred to each of their webs. For their first chapter, "The Times," they selected five topics from their web dealing with events in history. For their second chapter, "The Life," they selected ten topics from their web dealing with events in Dr. King's life. Figure 23 shows their selections for these first two chapters and for the final chapter.

Ms. Sturman and I introduced our idea for a final "Life and Times" chapter. We asked the children if they thought Dr. King had been affected by the times in which he lived. Overwhelmingly, they said that he was, providing numerous examples of the discrimination he faced. We also asked the children if they thought Dr. King had affected the times in which he lived. Again, the children agreed that he had, citing his active role in the civil rights movement. From this discussion we added to the plans we had already developed for the first two chapters. We were careful to provide questions but not answers.

While this framework is not exhaustive, it was challenging and manageable for fourth graders. It provided them with the direction and support they needed to keep them moving from topic to topic.

As they began writing, the children were able—even encouraged—to tell Dr. King's story the way they saw it. A look at what two students wrote about the Jim Crow laws illustrates the variety of narration and interpretation that occurred. The first student approached the topic by asking why, even after the Civil War, blacks were not free:

> The Civil War ended but blacks didn't have their freedom in the South. How come? How come blacks didn't have their freedom? Maybe it was the color of their skin. No, it couldn't be. People couldn't be that mean. But it's true, they were that mean.
> When the Civil War ended blacks were supposed to have their freedom, but in the South they didn't. The people separated everything, bathrooms, movie theaters, drinking fountains, all sorts of places. This was called segregation or Jim Crow laws.

A second student, in contrast, defined the Jim Crow laws and then asked the reader to reflect on them and make an evaluation:

> Jim Crow laws were in the South. They separated blacks from whites in public places like bathrooms, buses, hotels, restaurants, schools, and each other. What do you think about the Jim Crow laws from what you know? I knew the laws were bad as soon as I read about them.

Writing, conferencing, sharing, revising, illustrating—all of these activities became the center of our efforts for more than a month as the children followed our framework and prepared their biographies. At

Chapter I: The Times
  1. Jim Crow Laws
  2. Supreme Court Rules Segregation in Schools Unconstitutional
  3. Bus Boycott
  4. Children's Crusade
  5. March on Washington
Chapter II: The Life
  1. Early Years
      —Experiences with Jim Crow laws
      —Wasn't allowed to play with white friends
      —Experience at shoe store
  2. Adult Years
      —Learned about nonviolence (Gandhi's teachings)
      —Ordained as Baptist minister
      —SCLC—practiced nonviolence
      —Bus boycott
      —Marches: March on Washington
                Selma to Montgomery
  3. Honors
      —*Time* Magazine "Man of the Year"
      —Nobel Peace Prize
Chapter III: The Life and Times
  1. How did history affect Martin Luther King?
  2. How did Martin Luther King affect history?

Figure 23. A framework for a life-and-times biography.

the end of this time, every student had completed an original work, which was made into a book. The complete text of one fourth grader's life-and-times biography is included in Appendix C.

And what of the relationship between life and times? There was universal agreement among the children that each influenced the other. Here is a final example showing how one youngster described this relationship:

> Martin Luther King's life affected history. He changed the world. Before he was alive there was segregation. As Martin grew, the country grew. As Martin changed, the country changed. The blacks and whites formed a nation. When the life and times blended together, history changed and everyone changed. And because of Martin Luther King the world is a better place to live in.

Looking Back at the Life-and-Times Approach

Of all the classroom biography projects described so far, this one lasted the longest. We began in October and were still passionately involved and writing in June. This was largely due to our extended study of events that surrounded the struggle for civil rights. For instance, a study of the Supreme Court decision declaring segregation in schools unconstitutional prompted students to go to the library and search out the details of Linda Brown's experience. Similarly, a study of the bus boycott generated interest in looking at newspaper articles and biographies of Rosa Parks. Fortunately for us, Rosa Parks visited Brooklyn during the time we were studying about her, and we were able to look at newspaper reports describing her visit and her reflections on her dramatic past. Over and over again, our study of Dr. King's life generated an interest in learning about history. We simply could not understand his life without understanding the context of the times in which he lived.

This project gave children a subject they could care about deeply and passionately. To understand Dr. King, they were willing to read, write, speak, and listen. The study of his life taught them about the ugliness of hatred, bigotry, and prejudice, but it also taught them about the power of nonviolence, love, and determination. It taught them that in a less-than-perfect world there is always the possibility of change.

Going Further

One way to extend the life-and-times study described in this chapter is for children to consider how current events influence their own lives and the lives of people they know.

1. Using the format below, children can make time lines showing events in their own lives and events in history. Each child can consider the following questions for discussion: Which events in your life do you consider most significant? Which historical events that occurred during your lifetime do you consider most significant? Why?

Events in My Life	Year	Events in History

2. Children can look for current events that are making a difference in their lives. Are there events reported in the daily newspaper (e.g., changes in school policies, changes in the economy, new inventions and discoveries, new laws) that will make a difference in their lives? How? A bulletin board can be used to collect newspaper clippings of these current events.

3. Children can expand their individual time lines in order to make predictions about the future. What aspirations do they have for the future? What are their plans and goals for this year? Next year? Five years from now? What predictions do they have for local events? National events? World events?

4. Children can interview an adult about an important event in history that occurred during his or her lifetime. Children might begin by asking, What important event in history occurred during your lifetime? How did this event affect your life? The results of these interviews can be shared in class.

5. To further explore the life-and-times approach in nonfiction literature, the class can read books like Genevieve Foster's *Abraham Lincoln's World*. In this book, Foster describes events taking place all over the world during the span of Lincoln's lifetime. For example, at the time of Lincoln's birth, Napoleon dominated Europe, Bolívar conceived of a plan to liberate Venezuela, and Jefferson repealed a trade embargo that kept American ships from trading overseas. Other books by Foster that use the same approach explore the worlds of George Washington, William Penn, Captain John Smith, and Christopher Columbus.

The chapters in Part II have explained in-depth approaches to reading and writing biography. The final chapter suggests additional ways to keep alive children's enthusiasm for biographies.

8 Feeding an Interest in Biography

After completing one of the projects described in this book, one fourth grader wrote:

> I thought I would never finish or do well on this book. But I did. I did well and now I'm finishing my book. Now I feel that I'm doing great and I really am proud of my work.

This kind of enthusiasm, once kindled, needs to be supported by providing children with continued opportunities to read and respond to biographies. This chapter deals with that need by suggesting additional biography-centered activities. The chapter ends with a list of resources for teachers who want to learn more about biographies in order to develop their own programs.

Biography-Centered Activities

The activities suggested below are flexible enough to be used by individuals, small groups, or entire classes.

Becoming "Biography Buffs"

Since children are generally enthusiastic readers of series books like The Baby Sitters Club, Nancy Drew, or The Hardy Boys, why not introduce biography series? Children can read their way through "series" of biographies such as the Women of Our Time books (Viking Penguin), the Crowell Biography series (Crowell), the Childhood of Famous Americans series (Bobbs-Merrill), the Creative Minds books (Carolrhoda Books), and the Yearling Biographies (Dell). Readers can also compare and contrast the different series.

In addition, a "biography buff" can become a specialist in the works of various authors. Some of my favorite biographers whose works children can investigate are listed below:

Ingri and Edgar Parin d'Aulaire	Joe Lasker
Doris Faber	Milton Meltzer

Jean Fritz	F. N. Monjo
James Haskins	Robert Quackenbush
R. R. Knudson	Diane Stanley

Specialists can, of course, give specialty reports to the class.

Building Jackdaws

A jackdaw (Rasinski 1983) is a collection of material that adds to a reader's understanding and enjoyment of a book. It can consist of print or nonprint items that are gathered from home or the library or constructed by the reader. A jackdaw based on a biography can include materials such as the following:

a map showing the subject's travels

newspaper clippings

photographs

copies of speeches and letters

filmstrips

tapes of the subject or about the subject

explanations of vocabulary words found in the biography

diagrams

dioramas

illustrations

lists of other books about the subject

Groups of students can work together to build a jackdaw related to a particular biography. This material can then be shared with other groups of readers who are then invited to read the biography and examine the jackdaw.

Experimenting with Form

After reading a biography, invite readers to transform the information into a play, a newspaper article, an imaginary interview, a radio review, or a poem. The change in form will not only affect the length of the product, but also its meaning.

Discuss these changes. Does a play, for example, "stretch out" a particular incident reported in a biography? What details drop out? Which details assume importance? What type of details are emphasized in newspaper articles? In poems? Interviews? Reviews?

Deciding on the Best: Choosing Class Favorites

Just as adult organizations bestow awards on single books and on the collective works of one author, so can children (Johnson and Louis 1987). Individuals or committees can promote their favorite biography, telling why they think it deserves an award and even designing and presenting the appropriate award.

Awards can be given for the best biography in a particular category (athlete, scientist, explorer, etc.) or to the best biographer for a collection of work. When the award is given, the group should explain why this particular book or author was selected. In this way, children will be thinking about their criteria for judging the quality of the biographies they read.

Sharing Biographies across Grades

Something almost magical happens when older and younger children work together. They cooperate, discuss, and learn from each other.

Intermediate- and primary-grade children can read and discuss biographies together. An older child can interview a younger child and then select an appropriate biography to share. The pairs can read, discuss, and then write about the biography together.

Sources for Teachers

The following list of resources can be used to locate appropriate books for classroom projects. These resources can help you determine if there are enough books available for studying a particular subject.

Indexes

Usually found in the reference section of the library, these books list biographies (and books on other subjects) that are currently in print.

Best Books for Children: Preschool through the Middle Grades. 3d ed. John T. Gillespie and Christine B. Gilbert, eds. New York: R. R. Bowker, 1985.

> Lists and briefly annotates current biographies according to the following breakdown: historical and contemporary Americans; world figures; explorers and adventurers; scientists and inventors; artists, writers, composers, and performers; and sports figures. Contains an index of biographical subjects.

Children's Catalog. 15th ed. Richard H. Isaacson, Ferne E. Hillegas, and Juliette Yaakov, eds. New York: H. W. Wilson, 1986.

Annotations of biographies often include excerpts of reviews from periodicals such as *School Library Journal, Horn Book, New York Times Book Review,* and *Bulletin of the Center for Children's Books.*

The Elementary School Library Collection: A Guide to Books and Other Media. 14th ed. Lois Winkel, ed. Williamsport, Penn.: Brodart, 1988.

Lists and annotates individual and collective biographies. The listing integrates information about audiovisual material with information about books.

Her Way: A Guide to Biographies of Women for Young People. 2d ed. Mary-Ellen Siegel. Chicago: American Library Association, 1984.

Lists and annotates biographies of more than 1,100 women. Part I lists the selected women alphabetically, gives a short profile, and lists recommended biographies. Part II lists and annotates collective biographies of women.

Subject Guide to Children's Books in Print. New York: R. R. Bowker.

An annual publication that lists biographies but does not annotate them. Biographies are listed according to classes of persons (artists, authors, musicians, etc.) or as subheadings under broader subjects such as U.S., women, and blacks. Companion book to *Children's Books in Print.*

Professional Books

These books address issues that are particularly significant to teachers.

Beyond Fact: Nonfiction for Children and Young People. Jo Carr, ed. Chicago: American Library Association, 1982.

A collection of thought-provoking essays about nonfiction writing for children. The section devoted to biography includes Carr's essay "What Do We Do about Bad Biographies?" Also includes essays by biographers Milton Meltzer and F. N. Monjo.

Eyeopeners! How to Choose and Use Children's Books about Real People, Places, and Things. Beverly Kobrin. New York: Viking Penguin, 1988.

A very readable handbook about using nonfiction books with children. A chapter written especially for teachers describes ways to use nonfiction in the classroom. Section on biographies provides a number of teaching ideas based on the recommended books.

Portraits: Biography and Autobiography in the Secondary School. Margaret Fleming and Jo McGinnis, eds. Urbana, Ill.: National Council of Teachers of English, 1985.

Although addressed to secondary school teachers, the material can be adapted for use in the elementary school. For example, a chapter entitled "The Biography Kit" describes a plan for creating an imaginary subject and then writing this subject's biography.

Surveys of Children's Literature

A section or chapter in each of the following books deals with selecting and using biographies.

Children and Books. 7th ed. Zena Sutherland and May Hill Arbuthnot. Glenview, Ill.: Scott, Foresman, 1986.

Discusses biographies suitable for "Younger Readers," "Middle Group Readers," and "Older Readers." Contains an annotated list of collective and individual biographies.

Children's Literature in the Elementary School. 4th ed. Charlotte Huck, Susan Hepler, and Janet Hickman. New York: Holt, Rinehart and Winston, 1987.

Section on biography includes a thorough discussion of criteria for selecting and evaluating biographies, as well as a survey of biographical formats found in children's literature. Many suggested titles.

Literature and the Child. 2d ed. Bernice Cullinan. New York: Harcourt Brace Jovanovich, 1989.

Chapter on historical fiction and biography includes teaching ideas, activities for students, and profiles of authors, as well as an introduction to children's biographies.

Through the Eyes of a Child: An Introduction to Children's Literature. 2d ed. Donna E. Norton. Columbus, Ohio: Merrill, 1987.

Chapter on nonfiction includes discussion of criteria for evaluating biographies and a survey of biographies of explorers, political leaders, artists, scientists, sports figures, and "people who have persevered." Separate chapter entitled "Involving Children in Nonfiction Literature" discusses activities that can be used in conjunction with reading biographies. Includes ideas for creative dramatics.

Notable Children's Trade Books in the Field of Social Studies

This yearly list of recommended books includes a section of notable biographies. Published each April in *Social Education* and also available from the Children's Book Council.

References

Works Cited

Caro, Robert A. 1986. Lyndon Johnson and the Roots of Power. In *Extraordinary Lives: The Art and Craft of American Biography*, edited by William Zinsser. New York: American Heritage.

Clifford, James L. 1970. *From Puzzles to Portraits: Problems of a Literary Biographer*. Chapel Hill: University of North Carolina Press.

Cullinan, Bernice. 1989. *Literature and the Child*. 2d ed. New York: Harcourt Brace Jovanovich.

Edel, Leon. 1984. *Writing Lives: Principia Biographica*. New York: W. W. Norton.

Egan, Kieran. 1979. What Children Know Best. *Social Education* 43 (February): 130–39.

——— . 1983a. Children's Path to Reality from Fantasy: Contrary Thoughts about Curriculum Foundations. *Journal of Curriculum Studies* 15:357–71.

——— . 1983b. Social Studies and the Erosion of Education. *Curriculum Inquiry* 13 (2): 195–214.

——— . 1986a. Individual Development in Literacy. In *Literacy, Society, and Schooling: A Reader*, edited by Suzanne deCastell, Allan Luke, and Kieran Egan. Cambridge: Cambridge University Press.

——— . 1986b. *Teaching as Storytelling: An Alternative to Teaching and Curriculum in the Elementary School*. London, Ontario: Althouse Press.

Elliot, David L., Kathleen Carter Nagel, and Arthur Woodward. 1985. Do Textbooks Belong in Elementary Social Studies? *Educational Leadership* 42 (April): 22–24.

Gordon, Lyndall. 1985. T. S. Eliot. In *The Craft of Literary Biography*, edited by Jeffrey Meyers. New York: Schocken Books.

Huck, Charlotte S., Susan Hepler, and Janet Hickman. 1987. *Children's Literature in the Elementary School*. New York: Holt, Rinehart and Winston.

Johnson, Terry D., and Daphne R. Louis. 1987. *Literacy through Literature*. Portsmouth, N. H.: Heinemann.

Kendall, Paul M. 1965. *The Art of Biography*. New York: W. W. Norton.

Langer, Judith A., and Arthur N. Applebee. 1987. *How Writing Shapes Thinking: A Study of Teaching and Learning*. NCTE Research Report No. 22. Urbana, Ill.: National Council of Teachers of English.

Larkins, A. Guy, Michael L. Hawkins, and Allison Gilmore. 1987. Trivial and Noninformative Content of Elementary Social Studies: A Review of Primary

Texts in Four Series. *Theory and Research in Social Education* 15 (Fall): 299–311.

Lash, Joseph P. 1982. *Love, Eleanor: Eleanor Roosevelt and Her Friends.* New York: Doubleday.

Levstik, Linda. 1986a. The Relationship between Historical Response and Narrative in a Sixth Grade Classroom. *Theory and Research in Social Education* 14 (1): 1–19.

———. 1986b. Teaching History: A Definitional and Developmental Dilemma. In *Elementary School Social Studies: Research as a Guide to Practice,* edited by Virginia A. Atwood. Washington, D.C.: National Council for the Social Studies.

Lomask, Milton. 1986. *The Biographer's Craft.* New York: Harper and Row.

Malamud, Bernard. 1987. Long Work, Short Life. *Michigan Quarterly Review* 26 (Fall): 601–11.

Mariani, Paul. 1983. Reassembling the Dust: Notes on the Art of the Biographer. *New England Review and Bread Loaf Quarterly* 5: 276–96.

Matthews, Gareth. 1988. The Philosophical Imagination in Children's Literature. In *Imagination and Education,* edited by Kieran Egan and Dan Nadaner. New York: Teachers College Press.

McCullough, David. 1986. The Unexpected Harry Truman. In *Extraordinary Lives: The Art and Craft of American Biography,* edited by William Zinsser. New York: American Heritage.

Meltzer, Milton. 1986. Notes on Biography. *Children's Literature Association Quarterly* 10 (Winter): 172–75.

Monjo, F. N. 1975. Great Men, Melodies, Experiments, Plots, Predictability, and Surprises. *Horn Book* 51 (October): 433–41.

Nadel, Ira B. 1984. *Biography: Fiction, Fact and Form.* New York: St. Martin's Press.

Oates, Stephen B. 1986. Biography as High Adventure. In *Biography as High Adventure: Life-Writers Speak on Their Art,* edited by Stephen B. Oates. Amherst: University of Massachusetts Press.

Purves, Alan C. 1985. That Sunny Dome: Those Caves of Ice. In *Researching Response to Literature and the Teaching of Literature: Points of Departure,* edited by Charles R. Cooper. Norwood, N.J.: Ablex.

Rasinski, Timothy V. 1983. Using Jackdaws to Build Background and Interest for Reading. Paper presented at the annual meeting of the International Reading Association, Anaheim, Calif., May 2–6. ERIC Document No. ED 234 352.

Ravitch, Diane. 1985. *The Schools We Deserve.* New York: Basic Books.

Rosenblatt, Louise M. [1938.] 1983. *Literature as Exploration.* New York: Modern Language Association.

———. 1978. *The Reader, the Text, the Poem: The Transactional Theory of the Literary Work.* Carbondale, Ill.: Southern Illinois University Press.

———. 1985. The Transactional Theory of the Literary Work: Implications for Research. In *Researching Response to Literature and the Teaching of Literature: Points of Departure,* edited by Charles R. Cooper. Norwood, N.J.: Ablex.

Schlesinger, Arthur M., Jr. 1988. On Leadership. Introductory essay to *Mother Teresa*, by Joan Graff Clucas. New York: Chelsea House.

Tuchman, Barbara W. 1979. Biography as a Prism of History. In *Telling Lives: The Biographer's Art*, edited by Marc Pachter. Washington, D.C.: New Republic Books/National Portrait Gallery.

Veninga, James F., ed. 1983. *The Biographer's Gift: Life Histories and Humanism*. College Station, Tex.: Texas A&M University Press.

Westfall, Richard S. 1985. Newton and His Biographer. In *Introspection in Biography: The Biographer's Quest for Self-Awareness*, edited by S. H. Baron and C. Pletsch. Hillsdale, N.J.: Lawrence Earlbaum.

Woodward, Arthur, David L. Elliott, and Kathleen Carter Nagel. 1986. Beyond Textbooks in Elementary Social Studies. *Social Education* 50 (January): 50–53.

Zarnowski, Myra. 1986. Building Biographies: A Snapshot Approach. *Social Science Record* 26 (Fall): 54–56.

———. 1988. The Middle School Student as Biographer. *Middle School Journal* 19 (February): 25–27.

Children's Biographies Cited

Adams, Patricia. 1987. *The Story of Pocahontas, Indian Princess*. Illustrated by Tony Capparelli. New York: Dell.

d'Aulaire, Ingri, and Edgar Parin d'Aulaire. 1950. *Benjamin Franklin*. Garden City, N.Y.: Doubleday.

Faber, Doris. 1985. *Margaret Thatcher: Britain's "Iron Lady."* Illustrated by Robert Masheris. New York: Viking Kestrel.

Foster, Genevieve. 1944. *Abraham Lincoln's World*. New York: Charles Scribner's Sons.

Freedman, Russell. 1987. *Lincoln: A Photobiography*. New York: Clarion Books/Ticknor and Fields.

Fritz, Jean. 1969. *George Washington's Breakfast*. Illustrated by Paul Galdone. New York: Coward-McCann.

———. 1973. *And Then What Happened, Paul Revere?* Illustrated by Margot Tomes. New York: Coward, McCann and Geoghegan.

———. 1976. *What's the Big Idea, Ben Franklin?* Illustrated by Margot Tomes. New York: Coward, McCann and Geoghegan.

Knudson, R. R. 1985. *Babe Didrikson: Athlete of the Century*. Illustrated by Ted Lewin. New York: Viking Kestrel.

Lawson, Robert. 1939. *Ben and Me*. Boston: Little, Brown.

———. 1953. *Mr. Revere and I*. Boston: Little, Brown.

———. 1956. *Captain Kidd's Cat*. Boston: Little, Brown.

Meltzer, Milton. 1985a. *Betty Friedan: A Voice for Women's Rights*. Illustrated by Stephen Marchesi. New York: Viking Kestrel.

———. 1985b. *Dorothea Lange: Life through the Camera*. Illustrated by Donna Diamond. Photographs by Dorothea Lange. New York: Viking Kestrel.

———. 1986. *George Washington and the Birth of Our Nation*. New York: Franklin Watts.

Mitchell, Barbara. 1987. *Raggin': A Story about Scott Joplin*. Illustrated by Hetty Mitchell. Minneapolis: Carolrhoda Books.

Monjo, F. N. 1970. *The One Bad Thing about Father*. Illustrated by Rocco Negri. New York: Harper and Row.

———. 1971. *The Vicksburg Veteran*. Illustrated by Douglas Gorsline. New York: Simon and Schuster.

———. 1973. *Me and Willie and Pa: The Story of Abraham Lincoln and His Son Tad*. Illustrated by Douglas Gorsline. New York: Simon and Schuster.

———. 1973. *Poor Richard in France*. Illustrated by Brinton Turkle. New York: Holt, Rinehart and Winston.

———. 1974. *Grand Papa and Ellen Aroon: Being an Account of Some of the Happy Times Spent Together by Thomas Jefferson and His Favorite Granddaughter*. Illustrated by Richard Cuffari. New York: Holt, Rinehart and Winston.

———. 1974. *King George's Head Was Made of Lead*. Illustrated by Margaret Tomes. New York: Coward, McCann and Geoghegan.

———. 1975. *Letters to Horseface*. Illustrated by Don Bolognese and Elaine Raphael. New York: Viking Press.

Stanley, Diane. 1986. *Peter the Great*. New York: Four Winds Press.

Walker, Paul R. 1988. *Pride of Puerto Rico: The Life of Roberto Clemente*. New York: Harcourt Brace Jovanovich.

Appendix A
Fictionalized Biographies Written
by Fourth Graders

Young Benjamin Franklin

I am Benjamin Franklin's sister and I can tell you a few things about him. It all started January 17, 1706, with the birth of my brother Benjamin. He was the fifteenth of our father's and mother's seventeen children. One of the first events in a newborn baby's life is being carried in his father's arms. I was proud to show off my new baby brother.

As Ben got older our parents were trying to find him trades. Our father wanted him to be a soap, candle [and] dishmaker, and he would make other things. But he wasn't so happy about that because he was going to have to smell the disgusting smell of hot stale grease. He was going to have [to] sign a paper saying he would be an apprentice until he was 21. He wasn't so happy about that either. I felt badly for him.

What Ben really wanted to do was be a printer. He didn't mind being an apprentice as long as he could be what he really wanted to be. He had to work for James, our brother. And as I said before he had to sign papers.

James' part of the bargain was to give him food, shelter, and clothing. He was very annoying to James but I understood why. Ben wanted James to pay more attention to him and pay less attention to his work. But of course he wouldn't agree. He was getting sick of working for our brother.

He worked for seventeen years which he thought was long enough. He decided to start his own printing shop and I don't have to tell you once Ben decides to do something he does it! He decided to run away.

He went to N.Y. to get the equipment he would need to open his own print shop. After a while he went to Philadelphia where he met Debby, his future wife. He soon returned to open his shop. But it just was too hard to handle by himself. He went out to dinner one night with Debby and he showed her around his shop. He had known Debby for seven years and he finally asked for her hand in marriage. And she said Yes. I was proud and happy. I love Ben, My brother.

Benjamin Franklin's World of Adventures

I am a European scientist. I was Ben Franklin's friend who worked with Ben on his inventions for many years. I was there when Ben did the experiment about electricity. I was frightened that Ben would get a shock. My thinking was correct. Ben took the shock through his arms and body and was knocked unconscious. After he was up from his unconsciousness his big idea was that electricity and lightning were one and the same.

Long before Ben's experiment he was an apprentice to his brother James. He thought his brother was a bossy person. Ben did not like being told things and James did not like how Ben was acting.

Soon Ben ran away from Boston to Philadelphia at the age of 18. There Ben's life went on. Ben started a library in 1731. He also wrote a large book called *Poor Richard's Almanac*. He did this from 1732 to 1757. *Poor Richard's Almanac* is a book that tells his sayings and gives the weather forecasts.

He invented the bifocals in 1743 and a heating device. He also invented the Franklin armonica, a musical instrument. At the age of 23 Ben started a newspaper called the *Gazette*. He also invented the odometer. An odometer is an instrument to measure distance. In 1748 Ben retired from printing and worked on other things.

In 1775 Ben signed the Declaration of Independence. Some of it is Ben's own writing. The colonies did not want to be ruled by Great Britain, so the[y] went to war. They won their independence.

Ben was in a club called the Junto Club which started out as the Leather Apron Club. In that club there were blacksmiths, shoemakers, carpenters, and printers. All of them could join the club. In that club they talked about business. The name Junto means a group or society. That club started in 1743 and went on. Ben Franklin as I know him was a very busy man. Ben was so busy that when I called [on] him to see how he was getting along he was never in. He was probably writing some of his sayings. One of them was "Early to bed and early to rise makes a man healthy, wealthy, and wise."

I got to meet Ben's wife. She was a wonderful woman called Deborah Reed. She was very pretty. If Ben had not married Deborah, I would have. Deborah and Ben were very happy together and they loved each other very much. They lived happily every after.

Ben Franklin, Apprentice to a Printer

When Ben was 12, my father and he were looking for a trade for him to learn in business. But when they couldn't find any that suited Ben, my father suggested he come to work for me, his brother James, as an apprentice.

When he came to work for me, we made an agreement. His part of the bargain was to be loyal to me, keep my secrets, and work for me until he was 21. I kept my part of the bargain, but Ben didn't.

Ben was really irresponsible; he failed to remember that I was his boss and I didn't like his attitude. He did what he wanted to do and I didn't like it. That's why we didn't get along. When Ben was 17, he ran away to Philadelphia. That's how he didn't keep his end of the bargain.

Ben thought he knew it all, but he didn't. I really think it was inconsiderate of him to run away like that. If he would have stayed four more years, he wouldn't have had such a rough time getting his business started.

But he did become successful. After a few years Ben came back to Boston and showed off. I didn't think that was nice. In fact, if he does it again, I will ignore him forever. But there's one thing you should know. That is, Ben was the fool and I was the smart one.

There's one thing I don't understand. If Ben was that irresponsible and he wasn't too smart, how come he became so successful? I guess he wised up.

Ben did a lot of things. He wrote Poor Richard's Almanac, signed the peace treaty between the United States and England and much later signed the Constitution. Despite how poorly we got along, I was PROUD! of my little brother for doing all of those things.

Appendix B
Nonchronological Biographies
Written by Fifth Graders

George Washington
Commander-in-Chief

Who was the man who unlinked the chain between the U.S. colonies and Great Britain? He was George Washington, a man of great height, but very quiet, who was chosen to lead the Revolutionary War.

George was very upset when he was chosen to lead the American army. Most of the men were not that well dressed. When George saw his men he said, "Are these the men I'm supposed to defend America with?"

At first there was no hope for Washington's men. They kept on losing battle after battle. Then one battle gave them more hope about the war. They won the battle of Princeton. Carelessly, they lost Philadelphia. One battle, then a black spot on a clean white cloth.

Then a nightmare called winter came and 2,500 men died. Men were so cold their legs turned black as night. It got worse. The soldiers were going through famine. Then General Von Steuben came and turned the men into soldiers.

It was the first of spring. The hardship was over at last. They were fighting the war.

After all that they get a traitor Benedict Arnold. Everybody was amazed. George was surprised. It almost brought tears to his eyes.

Lafayette came to the aid of the American soldiers. Since they had the French, everybody thought they were bound to win.

It was 1781. It was the moment of truth. General Cornwallis at Yorktown was like a cat stuck in a tree because the American soldiers were surrounding Yorktown. A messenger came to tell them the British surrender. "We won," they cried. George was asked to become King of the new country. George refused. And that's why we have [a] president instead of a king. Another reason George didn't want to be king is that he thought if he were king there would be another war. Besides they just got rid of one king, why get another?

This is why George was prepared for commander-in-chief because he was strong. You need that because you don't want somebody weak for commander-in-chief because you had to look strong. He also had to ride about 12 to 14 hours [a day]. If you're not strong you might fall off.

Two of the most important lessons that prepared him for commander-in-chief were love of freedom and service to your country. His love of freedom was so strong that he left Mt. Vernon and his family both of which he loved dearly in order to fight. He felt his country was so important that he left everything he loved behind to serve his country.

Another lesson he followed was set by Roman General Cincinnatus. When he finished fighting he went back to his farm. After George finished fighting the Revolutionary war, he retired back to Mt. Vernon.

86

George was always prompt. George needed that because you can't be late for a battle. If you're late you can be killed.

Why I think George was not prepared.

George simply hated the wilderness. In fact while his soldiers camped out, he went to an inn. The inn was worse than the wilderness so naturally he went outside.

George was short-tempered when he was a boy. You don't want some[one] who says in a bossy voice, "Go into battle!"

George was lacking in self-confidence because women put him down. You need somebody who believes in himself so his soldiers would believe in him. It was a new job. He never was commander-in-chief and he was like a bird just learning to fly.

After all this unpreparedness, I have something nice to say. I think George was an extraordinary, very courageous man. If I were asked to take the position as commander-in-chief, I'd say yes, but I'd be the planner not the fighter.

George Washington as President

After the peace treaty was signed between the British and Americans, George became the president. He did what [was] best for people.

Some leaders wanted George Washington to become the king. But George refused. He knew what kind of power kings have and he didn't want to have that kind of power. And also, he didn't want to be called "Your Majesty" or "Your Excellency."

George became the president on February 4, 1789. He made New York City the capital. He hired Pierre L'Enfant to plan the new capital, Washington D.C.

George Washington made Thomas Jefferson the Secretary of State and Alexander Hamilton the Secretary of Treasury. Jefferson started the Democratic-Republican party. Hamilton started the Federalist Party.

While the English and French were fighting, Washington didn't help France because Washington thought that the U.S. didn't have enough power to fight the British and would end up being owned by the British again. People booed George Washington because he didn't help the French when they were in trouble because the French helped George Washington when he was in trouble during the Revolutionary War.

George Washington liked to go to parties, tea parties, and dances. He especially like[d] Martha's tea parties on Friday[s]. He really had fun at those parties.

On December 11, 1799 George went out for a horse ride. It started to rain. When he came back he was all wet. The next morning he had a cold. He called the doctor and told the doctor to bleed him. On the night of December 14, 1799 George Washington, "The Father of His Country," died.

I think George Washington's earlier life did prepare him to become president because he was strong and courageous. That made him prepared because the president had to face trouble. He had to have courage and he had to be strong.

He learned love of freedom from the Fairfax family. The love of freedom was important for him when he became president because then he would respect the country and try to do the best for it.

He showed self-control in overcoming his love for Sally Fairfax. He knew that Sally Fairfax was married to his best friend George Fairfax. Self-control was important because he had to deal with a lot of politicians and without self-control he would have never been the first president.

By marrying Martha Custis, George Washington took on family responsibilities [which] were to take care of Martha's children and the Custis farm.

When George Washington was in trouble he never ran away from his problems. He face[d] them with honesty. He was a nice and decent man.

He had much of what people thought a president should have. I think that if he wasn't the *first* president he would still be a great president. He had responsibilities, courage, strength, and self-control. He was not formally educated. I think he was a great president.

Appendix C
A Life-and-Times Biography
Written by a Fourth Grader

A Peaceful Hero

Chapter I: The Times

The Jim Crow Laws

Every day we saw people going to different signs marked "blacks" or "colored" and "whites". The blacks had to obey the rules. If they drank out of the white water fountain that would mean they were breaking a law. What was this called. This was called segregation. What did it mean? This meant that blacks were separated from public places and had to stay away from things marked "whites". How did the people feel? Blacks felt things were wrong. They felt things must change. They felt they should have his or her freedom into all areas. Most of all they felt that things should change.

One day Martin and his brother A.D. were coming back from a trip. They went on a train. The air was full of sunshine and happiness until they got down to the South again. Boom! The train conductor pulled the curtain closed so nobody would see them. How sad they felt, not wanted to be seen by the whites!

Segregated Schools

Ohhh, how much the white boys and girls learned in their schools with books, desks, and well-educated teachers. All the black boys and girls had was a broken down building with very few books, desks, and chairs. How could people be like that? It was so unfair. Well this is how it was. How could the blacks ever learn? Well they managed but it was very hard to get their education. How did it feel? It felt very sad, and the black children were impatient. This is what all segregated black schools were like. How terrible it felt, but they learned to live with it. Did the black children like it? Of course not, they wanted nice schools and more books. They wanted to learn the things the white children knew.

Linda Brown went to Monroe Elementary School, a school for blacks. This school was not in her neighborhood. She had to walk on a busy street with no sidewalks, or six miles in the tall grass that grew near the train tracks. Linda's father wanted her to go to the school in their neighborhood. It was a white school. Mr. Brown sued the Board of Education. The case finally went to the Supreme Court. Judge Warren ruled that school segregation was unconstitutional.

Finally in 1954 the Supreme Court ruled school segregation unconstitutional. The white people weren't happy about this but it was a law and the blacks got what they wanted. This is how schools became integrated.

Bus Boycott

It was the same old day again. Every day was the same. The Jim Crow laws kept on running day by day, but this day was a surprising day. Usually blacks got up when they were told to if the white section in the bus was full. A lady named Rosa Parks refused to give up her seat. This is how it happened.

One day a lady had just finished with a day's work and her legs ached. She went on the bus, paid her fare, and went to the section for blacks in the back of the bus. After a little while the bus came to a stop. A lot of white people came on. It got crowded. The white section was full. The bus driver stopped the bus and went to the back where the black section was. "Get up," he said. These blacks got up without fussing, but one lady just sat there and ignored him. Her name was Rosa Parks. She was taken to the police station, arrested, photographed, and fingerprinted.

The next day E.D. Nixon found out. He telephoned Martin Luther King, Jr. to tell him what had happened. Martin Luther King, Jr. was a man who was fighting for the blacks' rights. Nixon told him that one of our black citizens had been arrested because she refused to give up her seat to a white passenger.

The next day Rosa was let out of jail on bail. They all had a meeting at Martin's father's church in which he was co-pastor. The blacks were all thinking of a plan for Rosa Parks. Rosa Park's Reverend of her church and Martin's best friend, Ralph Abernathy, were there too; so was Nixon. The church was crowded. "Yes! That would be it," yelled Martin Luther King. "A Bus Boycott!"

Children's Crusade

The Children's Crusade march, in May 1963 was a very special march. Children over eight were allowed to march. Why did the children march? The children marched because they too wanted their freedom. When they marched, many were arrested. The jails were getting filled up so the police put the children in a cellar with only a concrete floor. More children marched the next day. Sometimes the police used dogs or fire hoses. Both times the children were hurt; some died. The police did understand that they wanted their freedom, but they weren't going to give it to them. The white people weren't fair.

One day the children marched with Martin Luther King, Jr. as their leader. Eugene "Bull" Connor said, "Let'm have it."

That time the police let the fire hoses hit them. The next day when they marched again the dogs were let loose, and clothes were ripped off the children. Some died. The next day when they marched Bull Connor yelled, "Let'm have it." The police stood still. "Let'm have it," he screamed. The police still wouldn't move. The blacks had won a victory.

March on Washington

Martin had planned a march on Washington on August 28, 1963. That's also when he recited his famous "I HAVE A DREAM" speech. "Amen," people would call out. People from all over the world came to march, from different states in North America, and even from different countries. This was a happy moment for Martin.

The people marched on August 28, 1963, just as it had been planned.

People marched for their rights, freedom, justice, and many white people marched for the blacks' freedom also.

They marched on all of Washington, D.C.

In this chapter I wrote about some of the events that happened during the time of Martin Luther King, Jr. Those events were the Jim Crow Laws, School Segregation, The Bus Boycott, Children's Crusade, and the March on Washington.

In the next chapter you'll read about the events that happened during Martin Luther King's life.

Chapter II: The Life

His Early Years

Martin Luther King, Jr. was born on January 15, 1929. He was named after his father "Martin Luther King, Sr." He had an older sister Christine, and as he grew up he had a younger brother, Alfred Daniel, whom they called A.D. for short.

Martin was a very lucky young boy to have a roof over his head and a family of his own. Martin also had some problems even when he was a very young boy. He was growing up in the South with segregation. Segregation kept young black boys apart from young white boys.

One day, Martin was supposed to play with his two white friends. They never came over to his house so Martin went over to theirs. Their mother answered the door. She said that Martin wasn't allowed to play with his white friends ever again from that day on. Martin ran home in tears. His mother explained to him about segregation. He really didn't understand but he did get used to it.

Segregation was almost everywhere you went in the South. Martin's father preached at Ebenezer Baptist Church. Martin knew that his father would put a stop to segregation.

One Sunday Martin had gone to church with his family as usual where his father preached. His father spoke so loudly and clearly about the words of "GOD." Martin said to his mother, "Mama, I'm gonna get me some big words when I grow up too." "Indeed you will Martin. Indeed you will," Mrs. King replied quietly.

Why did the white people do this [segregation]? Well, they did it to annoy the blacks, and they did it so that black people couldn't get their freedom.

One day Martin went with his father to buy shoes. "I'll be happy to serve you if you just move to the back of the store sir," the clerk politely said. "These seats are perfectly fine here. If you don't serve us here, you won't serve us at all," Mr. King said in his strong voice that made Martin feel good inside. Martin knew he wasn't going to get shoes today because Mr. King walked out of the shoe store.

Martin was a very intelligent young boy, for he started school at the age of four. Martin was also very smart.

One day Martin was talking with his friends at school. He was saying, "For my birthday I had 5 candles on my cake; one was for good luck." The teacher overheard and found out that Martin was only four years old. He had to wait two more years to go back to school.

Martin's life was very hard and very scary. It was hard to live in a world where they were judged by the color of their skin, and not by the content of their character. It was scary because of the phone calls the family had gotten threatening them. This was very hard on Martin too.

Adult Years

Now Martin has grown up and really understands what the word "segregation" means. He's already co-pastor of his father's church.

Martin, in his spare time reads the lectures of Mahatma Gandhi. He is the non-violent leader of India. He was fighting for his country's freedom, but never used violence. Martin was influenced by this great man. Mahatma Gandhi was fasting which means not eating. That's what he was doing to fight—GO FAST. That's very unusual. Yes, it is.

Some people think they are doing the right thing but . . .they are only risking their lives. Martin, however, didn't do that. He kept fighting—not with violence, but with non-violence. Isn't that hard? Well, not if you've been influenced by so many people, like his father, his mother, one principal of the school he went to, and Gandhi. These were very special people to Martin. That's why he was influenced by them.

Martin married a young girl, Coretta Scott, at her home in Alabama on June 18, 1953.

On their first date Coretta had doubts about Martin, but she still went out with him.

Martin came on strongly at their first date. Martin asked Coretta to marry him. Coretta almost said "NO" but she accepted. She accepted because she liked men who were fighting for their rights, other people's rights, and their freedom.

The King family moved down to Montgomery, Alabama when they had their first daughter "Yolanda" who they called "Yoki" as a nickname.

Remember the time Rosa Parks got arrested? Well, Martin Luther King did something about that. He formed a "Bus Boycott." The black leaders talked it over one evening in Martin's father's church. They all had thought of it. The girls and women would make copies of the paper that said something like— "NO ONE BLACK RIDE BUSES TOMORROW, DEC. 5, 1955. ALL DUE TO ROSA PARKS' ARREST."

So, the next day Martin and Coretta were up before sunrise. "Corey," Martin called, "the buses are empty!"

Martin, for the rest of the day, went around the city. Only eight blacks were all Martin saw throughout the whole day on the buses during the Bus Boycott. The bus boycott lasted 381 days.

There was a special march that Martin Luther King had formed. He knew that children wanted peace in the world too, so he formed the Children's Crusade in 1963. Children over eight were allowed to march. A principal of one school locked his gates so the children wouldn't get out, but they climbed over the locked gates and joined the march. The black children, including Dr. King were singing songs, and holding up signs. Nothing would stop them now— nothing.

In 1957, Martin Luther King went to New York. When he was there he went to a department store. While he was walking around, a lady stopped him. She was a black lady. Politely she said, "Are you Martin Luther King?" "Yes," Martin replied. "I've been looking for you." Then—she stabbed him. If Martin would have sneezed or coughed he would have died. Martin didn't want the lady to get arrested, so he said, "Put her in a hospital to get help."

In 1957, Martin and the King family moved back to Atlanta, Georgia. He wanted to be with his family again, and he wanted to see how things were going.

Pretty soon Martin and Coretta had another child, Martin Luther King. They called him "Marty" for short.

When he was in Atlanta, he was co-pastor of his father's church, the Ebenezer Baptist Church. When he was back down in Montgomery he was pastor of the Dexter Avenue Church.

Martin was going to Memphis, Tenn. to see how things were going. As he was walking down the streets he saw blacks working in the heat. Martin was furious about this. He knew he had to do something about it. When he was walking he saw black boys throwing rocks into the windows of white stores. They screamed out "I want my freedom!"

Martin went back to Atlanta. In about a week or two he went back up to Memphis again. He stayed at the Lorraine Hotel. At about 5:58 Martin went into the hotel to get a sweater, because it was getting chilly out. When he stepped out on the balcony—in less than 5 seconds a shot went off. Martin Luther King, Jr. was shot. He was assassinated in April when he had planned the "Poor People's March." He was carried in the wagon that he was going to be using in that march.

The march went on, but it still wasn't same without Martin.

James Earl Ray shot Martin. He was found and arrested.

Honors

Dr. Martin Luther King won a lot of honors. He won the Nobel Peace Prize in 1963, for leading non-violent demonstrations. He was "Man of the Year" in TIME magazine in 1963, but he got this wonderful award in 1964. He was awarded $50,000 along with the Nobel Peace Prize. He received this prize in Oslo, Norway. He donated this money to a black association.

We honor this great man every year on January 18, by giving him a National Holiday.

Chapter III: Life and Times

"History Affects Martin"—"Martin Affects History"

How did History affect Martin? Well, when he was young the Jim Crow laws started affecting him by not letting him play with his white friends, and not letting him go to the same schools as the white children did, and not letting him go to the same amusement parks as the white children did. This was hard on Martin.

As he got a little older history started affecting him more. Martin started leading non-violent marches like the Children's Crusade and the March on Washington in 1963, and the Selma to Montgomery March in 1965. Martin was involved in so many things—like being elected president of the S.C.L.C. (Southern Christian Leadership Conference). He was being trusted to help the world.

Martin made speeches that affected history. As he spoke people understood more clearly what Martin had meant about segregation to blacks. People started understanding how the black people felt. Every time the white people heard these speeches it gave them a bad feeling that what they had done was wrong.

The words of Martin Luther King were starting to come alive. Every day things started changing because of the words of Martin. Martin knew that one day things would change for good and forever.

"I have a dream that one day my four little children will live in a world where they will not be judged by the color of their skin, but by the content of their character. I have a dream today!" The dream was coming alive. Martin had changed a country and a world. Most of all he had made peace.

We will all remember Martin for a long, long time.

Author

Myra Zarnowski is an assistant professor of education at Queens College, CUNY, where she teaches courses in language arts, children's literature, and social studies. She has contributed articles to journals such as *Language Arts, The Reading Teacher, The Social Studies, Social Science Record, English Record,* and *The Middle School Journal.* Professor Zarnowski is currently a member of the joint committee of the National Council for the Social Studies and the Children's Book Council that each year develops the list "Notable Children's Trade Books in the Field of Social Studies."